A creative study of the book of Ezra

A creative study of the book of Ezra

by Sheila Corey

Illustrated by Scott Angle

Standard Publishing
Cincinnati, Ohio

TABLE OF CONTENTS

Cover Illustration by Scott Angle
Cover and inside design by Dina Sorn
Edited by Dale Reeves

Library of Congress Cataloging-in-Publication Data:
Corey, Sheila, 1963-
   Rock the house : a creative study of the Book of Ezra / by Sheila Corey ; illustrated by Scott Angle.
      p.   cm.
   ISBN 0-7847-0770-7
   1. Bible. O.T. Ezra—Commentaries.
   2. Bible. O.T. Ezra—Study and teaching.
   3. Youth—Religious life. I. Title.
   BS1355.3.C645   1998
   222'.7'00712—dc21   97-49915
                                  CIP

© 1998 by Standard Publishing
All rights reserved
Printed in the United States of America

The Standard Publishing Company,
Cincinnati, Ohio.
A Division of Standex International Corporation.

05   04   03   02   01   00   99   98

5   4   3   2   1

How to Use This Book

In Matthew 12:43-45, Jesus shared an illustration of a demon finding a clean, empty house. The owner, thinking he had secured the house, due to its clean and well-kept appearance, would soon find out that his security system was faulty. Because the house was not occupied by God and his Word, the demon brought his buddies, and they were able to move in, leaving the house worse than before. Many of our youth are the misguided owners. They have a false sense of security in the world and have become complacent to sin. Therefore, when we teach about sin and its consequences, it seems to fall on deaf ears. Although Ezra is an Old Testament book, its message of sin and salvation is very clear. A humbled nation of Judah had returned from exile to rebuild the temple—only to find that it was their "inside temple" that needed to be restored. The confrontation with their own sin, through the spiritual guidance of Ezra, brought the people to their knees—ready to rid their lives of sin and to build a relationship with God.

The six lessons and bonus session in *Rock the House* are designed to compare the rebuilding of the temple in Ezra's time to the temple in which God lives today—Christians. Just like the Israelites, teenagers today need to be taught not only to recognize sin, but to rid themselves of it in order to get their "house" clean. In doing this they soon realize this task cannot be done alone. Complete ownership of the house must be given to God (Hebrews 3:6). Even though getting rid of sin is not a self-cleaning process, youth can learn to despise the sins in their lives, remove the bad habits that are causing them to sin and learn to run from it. We also can teach our youth to replace the sins with godly thoughts and actions that will help them with the maintenance of their house.

Use these lessons to help your teens desire for Christ to "clean house" of their sin and to know how to remodel, so they can have a temple worthy to be occupied by the living God.

Each lesson is divided into four parts: **Laying the Foundation**—a lesson commentary on each of the Scriptures used; **Sketching the Design**—a brief opener that helps teens begin to get a *smell* of what the lesson is about; **Studying the Blueprint**—a time for students to *taste* what God has to say through his Word; and **Remodeling the**

Acknowledgments

- To the Corey family, Marty, Wesley and Leisha. Thanks for being my cheering section.

- To Dale Reeves, editor, for believing in this project and for publishing powerful youth materials.

- To my Eastview family. Your constant encouragement and prayers kept me writing. (Special thanks to Marla Scherle, Lisa Shireman and Deb Schoolcraft for everything!)

- To the high school youth at Eastview Christian Church, past and present, for being good listeners and doers. You have taught me in more ways than one. (Special thanks to Chad Heathco for the illustration and Dave Baysinger for sharing your wisdom.)

- To Terry Harmon, a great youth minister. Thanks for the resources and allowing me to continue to teach.

- To Kathi Isbell, for heading me in the right direction.

Interior—a time for students to apply or *chew on* what they just learned. Each section presents more than one option from which you can choose to build your lesson. Always keep in mind the personalities, needs and learning styles of your students as you plan each session. At the conclusion of each study, be sure to distribute copies of the reproducible devotional guide, **The Midweek Clean**, to encourage your teenagers to dig into God's Word during the week.

PRESS ON!

Teaching teenagers takes commitment. At times we can get discouraged because we see their ups and downs. There have been times when I taught a lesson and thought I bombed because I received absolutely no response. Then at a later time, I heard a teenager give a lesson or a devotion and the same biblical truth that was in my lesson was repeated. Teenagers respond according to what is happening around them. For instance, if it is prom week, they may be extra hyper (even if they are not the ones going)! If it is test week, they may be quiet or stressed. Train yourself to know what is happening in your teens' lives and vary the lessons accordingly (if it is test week, you might want to lighten your lesson so it is not too heavy; if it is prom week, you might want to do a more active lesson). But do not judge your teaching ability according to their responses (unless it is constant boredom), for they are soaking in more than you realize.

For several years I struggled with whether or not I was making a difference in their lives. I felt like quitting. I shared this privately with one of the teens in my group, who is now the lead singer of the Christian alternative group *Bleach* (can you tell that I am proud of him?). He said something to me that has forever changed my views on teaching.

"Do you believe that God speaks through you when you teach?" he asked.

I said, "Yes, when I prayerfully consider what God wants me to say."

His reply was, "Who better to teach us than God himself?"

It is not our *ability* to teach that makes a difference, but our *availability* to be molded and used by God. He speaks when we get out of the way and let him be heard. If you have prayerfully considered that teaching teens is how God wants to use you, then press on!

Rock the House

Clip Art Promo Page

970 B.C.	Solomon becomes king of 12 tribes of Israel.
966-959 B.C.	Solomon builds the first temple in the city of Jerusalem.
930 B.C.	Civil War—12 tribes of Israel divide. The 10 northern tribes are known as Israel and the two southern tribes are known as Judah.
722 B.C.	Assyrians invade the northern kingdom, scattering the people. Some tribes migrated south.
586 B.C.	Babylon invades the southern kingdom, destroying the temple and exporting the people to Babylon.
537 B.C.	The first return of exiles under Zerubbabel.
516 B.C.	The restoration of the temple is stopped, then completed.
458 B.C.	The second return of exiles under Ezra.
445 B.C.	The third return of exiles under Nehemiah to build the wall.

THE INSIDE SCOOP ON THE BOOK OF EZRA

EZRA: THE MAN WITH MANY HATS

- His name means "help" (something the Israelites needed lots of).

- He wrote the book of Ezra (which covers 81 years of Israelite history beginning with their return from captivity).

- He was a scribe (a writer, translator, interpreter and keeper of God's Word and public documents).

- He put together what is known today as the Old Testament canon, (the collection of Old Testament books).

- He loved to read God's Word to others (Nehemiah 8:2, 3, 18) and enjoyed helping others pray (Ezra 8:21; 9:1–10:1).

- He was an enabler. He knew God's Word, recognized sin and used that knowledge to guide others back to God.

MEET THE CONSTRUCTION CREW IN THE BOOK OF EZRA

ZERUBBABEL: He led the first group of 50,000 Jews back to Jerusalem. He was designated by God to lead the people to rebuild the temple.

JESHUA: He was a high priest, also designated by God to rebuild the temple and restore the Jews back to God.

HAGGAI AND ZECHARIAH: They were prophets of God whose preaching and prophecies motivated the Jews to continue rebuilding after the work had stopped for 10 years. Their words are recorded in the Old Testament books bearing their names. The book of Zechariah contains some cool prophecies about Christ.

WRECKING, REMODELING AND RELOCATION

LAYING THE FOUNDATION

2 CHRONICLES 36:14-23

The Israelites really blew it this time. God had given them every chance, throughout their history, to be faithful to him. Instead, they chose to worship other gods, "defiling the temple." Since they chose not to obey God, he allowed Jerusalem and the temple to be destroyed. The Israelites were carried into captivity to Babylon (586 B.C.), a pagan world, where there was no worship of the one true God. Sometimes we do not realize the value of a possession until it is lost.

EZRA 1:1–2:1

For 49 years Jerusalem's temple lay in ruins. In God's timing, Babylon was overthrown by King Cyrus of Persia. God moved the heart of this pagan king to allow the remnant of Israelites to return to their homeland to rebuild what their sin had destroyed. These verses describe the king's edict for the first group of Israelites to return to Jerusalem to rebuild the temple. Often our lives lie in ruins but, amazingly, God can use anyone, sometimes moving the heart of an unbeliever, to bring us to him. He wants us close to him and will use any avenue that can accomplish his purpose.

2 CHRONICLES 6:18-21

Solomon was amazed at the fact that God would choose to allow his presence to reside in a man-made structure on earth when his dwelling place is Heaven. God's love, overriding human logic, came close to man by manifesting his presence in the Holy of Holies of the temple.

Solomon humbly realized that he did not deserve God's presence in the temple for he and his nation were sinful. In the same way, we should be in awe that God would be willing to live inside us.

1 CORINTHIANS 3:16, 17

The death and resurrection of Jesus Christ changed the dwelling place of God's Spirit. When Jesus died, the temple curtain was torn to indi-

LESSON TEXT
Ezra 1:1–2:1; 1 Corinthians 3:16, 17

LESSON FOCUS
"God's temple is sacred, and you are that temple." (1 Corinthians 3:17)

LESSON GOALS
As a result of participating in this lesson, students will:

- Discover the background that put the Israelites into exile and what allowed them to return to rebuild the temple.
- Compare themselves as the temple of God to Solomon's temple.
- Grasp the fact that God's presence lives inside those who are Christians.
- Realize they must become the kind of house in which God can live.

Check This . . .
To help your students find Ezra, try the following method. Put your thumb in the middle of your Bible. You should be at the book of Psalms or close to it. Go backwards four books from Psalms and you have Ezra. Any books before the five books of poetry are history (past). Any books after the books of poetry are prophecies (future).

Check This . . .
Sometimes the Old Testament can be intimidating to read. *Halley's Bible Handbook,* by H. H. Halley (Zondervan), and *The Books of History,* by James E. Smith (College Press), are helpful resources.

Check This . . .
Just for fun, read a shortened version of *The Three Little Pigs.* Ask, **"If you were to compare the pigs' houses as if each represented a relationship with God, what would each house represent?"**

Materials needed:
A bottle of bubbles/wand; a game board; cards; a Super-Soaker water gun (water optional)

Check This . . .
For more information on how to pull off an effective impromptu skit, check out Youth Specialties' *Spontaneous Melodramas* (Zondervan Publishing).

cate God's Spirit was no longer going to reside in the temple in Jerusalem. He had changed residence. Christians are now the temple of God. It is only by the purification of our sins through Jesus Christ that we become the dwelling place of God! Wow, what an amazing love!

SKETCHING THE DESIGN

THE HUMAN HOUSE

Divide your students into three groups. Ask, **"If you were a building, how would you build yourself? What materials would you use? Would you be warm and welcoming or cold and drafty? Would you be easily destroyed or would you stand firm through the storms?"** Instruct each group to build its house using themselves as the building material. Have them designate one person as the realtor who will sell the house. The realtor needs to describe the house, what it is constructed of, and why it is worth buying.

Conclude this activity by asking, **"Have you ever thought of yourself as a house? Most people have heard they are a creation of God, but few would admit they are a house. In the Old Testament times, God lived in a house, called a temple, that was built by King Solomon around 960 B.C. People worshipped God there until the Babylonians destroyed it in 586 B.C. The book of Ezra tells the story about the rebuilding of God's temple and the restoration of his people, the Israelites."**

TO MAKE A LONG STORY SHORT

This is an impromptu skit that is to be read aloud to your students. They will act out the parts you assign them as they hear their parts read. No practice is required. The only preparation needed is to practice reading the skit a few times to get a feel for the story. This skit provides your students an abbreviated version of the history of Israel in an amusing, interactive way. It is not intended to be biblically accurate, only to teach biblical truths allegorically. If you do not have enough people, have the "actors" play more than one part or have only two people play the 12 tribes (one for northern tribes; one for southern tribes). The roles needed are as follows: Abraham (1 person); Abraham's 12 grandsons/12 tribes of Israel (12); King Solomon (1); temple of Solomon (2); God (1); the wives of Solomon (2); king of Assyria (1); king of Babylon (1); king of Persia (1); and Jesus (1).

Choose your actors before class begins. Tell them that when they hear their part, they should act accordingly. That means they'll have to listen closely to the story!

"About 2,000 years after the creation of the world and 400 years after the flood lived a man named Abraham. God said to him, 'Hey Abe, hit the road and I, yes only I, will make you into a great nation.' Abraham was so pleased that he began to <u>dance</u> a long, long, long way to the land of Canaan. There he had 12 grandsons.

The sons and their descendants began to multiply like rabbits. After many years of emptying their sandals of desert sand, the sons were eventually given their own section of land because their feet stunk and they couldn't control their bodily noises. They became known as the 12 tribes of Israel.

Many years later, the 12 tribes (alias Israelites) had a wise king named Solomon, who looked similar to the statue, 'The Thinker' (one fist on the forehead and one arm behind the back) **because he was very wise. Wise King Solomon had the Israelites** <u>build</u> **a beautiful temple in the city of Jerusalem** (have the "temple" stand facing each other with their hands together) **where God's presence sat inside.** (Have "God" sit inside the temple.)

The people were so awed at the fact that God would choose such a humble abode that they would sit around the temple for hours to worship him. All the people would <u>wave</u> their arms up and down and say slowly in their native tongue, 'O - wha - tagoo - siam. O - wha - tagoo - siam.' Realizing the awesomeness of God, they would say it faster and faster and faster (when said faster it comes out, "Oh what a goose I am"). **God really loved all this attention; to show his approval, he blessed them by blowing bubbles on them.** (Have "God" blow bubbles.)

Years later King Solomon grew tired of being wise all the time. He stopped standing like 'The Thinker' and decided he would play the leading role in the movie, 'Dumb and Dumber.' He began marrying women from other lands that worshiped many gods. They also had bad habits like not shaving their armpits and watching syndicated talk shows. He did not marry just one woman! He married 700 women at the same time, later buying stock in the local deodorant company.

Solomon was so busy with his wives that he didn't notice that his nation was lapsing in their worshiping and chanting. The people occasionally would worship at the temple, but then would sneak into the bathroom and play games like 'Poker' and 'Dung Pits and Dragons.' God had X-ray vision, seeing through the walls; he did not like the games the Israelites played. He was pretty ticked at Solomon and the Israelites, so he stopped blowing blessed bubbles from the temple. The Israelites were so busy playing games that they did not notice how upset God had become. They did not even hear God yelling from the temple, 'Hey, dummies! Wake up and smell the coffee.' Yet, the Israelites, who did not even like coffee, did not listen.

Many years later, the Israelites became angry at each other. Ten tribes wanted to play 'Dung Pits and Dragons' and two tribes wanted to play 'Poker.' There was a civil war, and the tribes divided. Ten tribes went north and two tribes went south, still playing their games in their own country. Without God blowing blessed bubbles, both the northern tribes and the southern tribes became easy prey for all the other nations (the audience) **to pick on. They would call**

Check This . . .
Before starting this series, take the time to do a quick study with your students on Solomon's temple. Have them create a small scale model of the temple using popsicle sticks, glue, paint and cardboard. The description is found in 1 Kings 1-8 and 2 Chronicles 1-7.

them names like 'Dragon Lips' and 'Dirty Dealers.' Eventually the king of Assyria, who looked sort of like Arnold Schwarzenegger, seized the 10 tribes and drove them out of the north, scattering the people all over and confiscating their game board. The king of Babylon, a big baby who cried and threw temper tantrums, invaded the southern nation, destroying the temple (after the presence of God had already left), beating up their king and poking out his eyes. Then he <u>carried</u> the two tribes off to Babylon where they lived in captivity. For 70 years God stood and watched, shaking his head in sadness, holding onto the blessed bubble blower and wishing he could blow bubbles.

The northern nation never became its own Jewish nation again, but the southern nation returned to Jerusalem when the king of Persia beat up the king of Babylon and took over his country. The exiles returned, realizing how much they really blew it by playing stupid games. They rebuilt the temple where God's presence once more lived and blew blessed bubbles. And the Jewish nation again chanted, 'O - wha - tagoo - siam' until 400 years later when God's Son came to earth to 'clean house' with a Super-Soaker." (Have Jesus jump out with the water gun.)

STUDYING THE BLUEPRINT

OPEN HOUSE!

Distribute writing utensils and copies of the student sheet on page 14. Have students pair off, then read the verses and answer the questions together. After they have finished, encourage input on the first question. Then ask for volunteers to read the Scriptures and discuss the questions. Close by saying, **"God wants to live inside us, but we have to be open to him. In what kind of house can God live? Are you that kind of house? What kind of house will you build for him?"**

CLEAR THE AREA! WRECKING BALL!

Ahead of time, cut out the four blocks of type from the student sheet. Divide your students into four groups. Give each group one block. Begin by saying, **"When some people purchase an older house, they need to remodel a room or two. Some houses, depending on the upkeep on the house, need to be completely restored. Read the verses assigned to your group, determine the condition of God's house and why it needed to be restored."**

Allow a spokesperson from each group to report back to the other three groups.

Materials needed:
Reproducible student sheet on page 14 of this book; writing utensils

Materials needed:
Reproducible student sheet on page 15 of this book; scissors

REMODELING THE INTERIOR

WHO IS MAN?

Ask, **"What is man that God would even pay any attention to him? He is the Creator and we are the created. Because of what Jesus did on the cross, an incredible change occurred! God chose man to be his temple. Why? Because he loves us and desires to be close to us. Our part is to give God complete ownership of our lives and allow him to cleanse and mold us into what he desires us to be. What kind of dwelling will you build to house the Creator of the universe?"**

Read 2 Chronicles 6:18-21 as a closing prayer. When you come to verse 20, instruct each student to dub in verbally his or her name after the word "temple," then continue through verse 21.

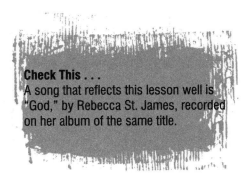

Check This . . .
A song that reflects this lesson well is "God," by Rebecca St. James, recorded on her album of the same title.

REFLECTION

Begin this activity by saying, **"God is like this flashlight; he is the light to a darkened world. We are like this mirror that reflects his presence inside us. Sometimes our mirror is spiritually dirty or foggy and does not reflect God's presence in its true light."** Put the black paper over the mirror and continue. **"Sometimes—either because God does not live inside us at all, or we choose to let sin rule over us—we do not reflect God's presence at all."** Pass out small pieces of colored paper to students. Have them write down their answers to the following questions:

- **On a scale to 0 to 10 (0 being without Christ and 10 being a perfection reflection of God), where do you stand as a reflection of God's presence?**
- **Where would you like to be?**

Close by asking God to guide each "temple" to be a true reflection of the presence of God.

Materials needed:
Mirror; black construction paper; flashlight; colored paper; writing utensils

SANCTUARY

Close by singing the chorus "Sanctuary." If your teens do not know this, have someone musically inclined come and teach it to them. This would be a good closing song after each of the lessons in this study. The words are as follows:

Lord prepare me, to be a sanctuary,
pure and holy, tried and true.
With thanksgiving, I'll be a living, Sanctuary, for You.

Close by asking God to guide each "temple" to be a living sanctuary to house the presence of God. Distribute copies of **The Midweek Clean** to your students.

Materials needed:
The chorus "Sanctuary," recorded on *America's 25 Favorite Praise and Worship Choruses, Volume 4*; CD or tape player

OPEN HOUSE!

Your great uncle died and because he loved you so much, he left you $500,000. What kind of house would you buy and why?

___ A log cabin in the mountains of Colorado
___ A condo on the beach
___ A country fixer-upper with a white picket fence
___ A penthouse apartment in New York City
___ A ranch with horses
___ A farm

WHAT KIND OF HOUSE WOULD GOD BUY?

Look up 2 Chronicles 2:1-6; 6:18-21 and Acts 7:47-50.

In King Solomon's day, where did God choose to "dwell with men"?

Could God be confined to a cedar and stone structure?

Why did he choose to dwell in this man-made structure?

Look up 2 Chronicles 36:14-20.

Why was this structure destroyed?

Look up Ezra 1:1-5.

Why did God have the people in Ezra's day rebuild it?

Look up 1 Corinthians 3:16, 17.

What type of house does he want to live in today?

Look up Revelation 5:9.

What was the purchase price?

Look up 1 Corinthians 6:19.

Who is the owner of our house?

14 **Lesson 1**

CLEAR THE AREA! WRECKING BALL!

2 Chronicles 2:1-6; 6:18-21

CONSTRUCTION

• What was built, who was the builder and who dwelled there?

• Was God limited to this building? (Acts 7:48-50)

• If God could dwell anywhere, why do you think he chose to live there?

2 Chronicles 36:14-23

EVICTION

• Who destroyed God's house?

• What was its condition?

• What was the reason for its condition?

Ezra 1:1–2:1

REMODELING

• Who ordered the remodeling on God's house?

• Who was in control of the order?

• Who carried out the orders?

1 Corinthians 3:16-17

RELOCATION

• Where did God relocate his presence?

• Why did he relocate his presence?

• What should be the condition of his property before he can reside there?

• What was the purchase price? (Revelation 5:9)

The Midweek Clean
A Guide for Remodeling the Interior

Something to Read

Take a few moments to reread Ezra 1:1–2:1.

Something to Think About

In verses one and five, whose hearts had to be moved before God could work?

What is our spiritual heart? What does it mean for God to move a heart?

How important is our attitude and willingness to be molded in order to be changed by God?

King Cyrus was not a Jew, yet God used him in his plan to rebuild the temple and reestablish the Jews in Jerusalem. Sometimes God uses the most unusual methods to get close to us.

Can you name a "nonreligious" way that God used to get your attention?

Something to Do

Take a minute to think about what you would change in your bedroom in order to improve it.
Would you paint the walls? Put up wallpaper? Pick up your dirty socks?
What would it take to change it? Money, time, effort?
To change something, you have to act. Verse five states that the Israelites prepared themselves before they built the temple.
Write down three actions that you can do today to prepare yourself to be a temple worthy to house the living God.

1. _____

2. _____

3. _____

What will you have to change in your life to accommodate God?

"... everyone whose heart God had moved—prepared to go up and build the house of the LORD in Jerusalem."

Ezra 1:5

MISSED NAIL— HURT THUMB

LAYING THE FOUNDATION

EZRA 3:1-6

After the Israelites settled, they realized they needed to build something to protect them from the surrounding people. We would assume they would build a wall or some kind of weapon. Yet their first step was to build an altar. How would an altar protect them? It was less than 70 years ago that they had been a top-dog nation with a wall and a beautiful temple. But because they compromised God's truth, they became separated from God and they fell. They knew their greatest protection was God himself, and they knew they had better make things right with him. The only way to do that was to follow his Word and the guidelines he had established. There is a saying, "The Bible will either keep you from sin or sin will keep you from the Bible." Captivity caused them to see their sin through God's eyes. They understood the value of God's truth. For when we go against God's truth, flawless and without fault, we sin.

EZRA 3:7-13

The Israelites prepared themselves spiritually for six months before they began to rebuild. Their first project was to lay the foundation on top of the original foundation of the temple of Solomon that had been destroyed. At its completion they immediately began to praise God for the foundation! They not only praised God because this was a great accomplishment under the circumstances, but it also symbolized a new beginning for them. They were finally putting in proper perspective who they were (sinners) and who God is (sovereign). They realized their great need for God and had a desire to be close to him. This foundation symbolized the greatest step in a restored relationship with the Creator. Our foundation should also reflect the same: realizing who we are (sinners) and who God is (sovereign), then activating the desire to follow the Creator's Word.

2 TIMOTHY 2:19-21

"God's solid foundation" that stands firm is the truth of his Word. On

LESSON TEXT
Ezra 3

LESSON FOCUS
"The foundation of the LORD's temple had not yet been laid." (Ezra 3:6)

LESSON GOALS
As a result of participating in this lesson, students will:
- Discover that the Israelites returned from captivity a humbled nation—ready to build the foundation of the temple and their lives on God's Word.
- Recognize that when they go against God's blueprint, the Bible, they sin; and sin does not go unpunished.
- Confront the sins in their lives that are separating them from God.
- Understand that without the foundation of truth found in Jesus Christ, living a good life in an ungodly world is impossible.

that foundation is inscribed, "The Lord knows those who are his." He knows who are his because they are the ones who follow his Word, confess the name of the Lord and have turned away from wickedness. Our spiritual foundation on which to build is God's truth of who he is and what he says in his Word.

1 CORINTHIANS 3:10-18

The *Life Application Bible* footnote to this verse suggests: "Two sure ways to destroy a building are to tamper with the foundation and to build with inferior materials."[1] God has already provided a foundation for us to build our lives upon, that is, Jesus Christ—for he is "'the way and the truth and the life'" (John 14:6). Building on anything else will lead to sure destruction. We need to take seriously the building of our lives and be choosy about the construction materials we use. Popularity, acceptance from others, fame and money are generic materials that will not last. If we try to cut costs and fail to follow the blueprint (God's Word), it may also cost us our spiritual lives. For whatever we build with will be tested; if it is not of God, it will be destroyed. God says whoever destroys his temple, he will destroy.

ROMANS 1:20-32

This Scripture says that man is without excuse when it comes to sin because God has revealed himself in what he has created. Man chooses to exchange the truth of God and his Word to live the life of a lie. This Scripture passage explains why God allowed the Israelites to go into captivity and lose everything they had in Jerusalem. In reading verse 28, we can picture God throwing his hands up in the air, and saying, "All right, do what you want, but you will be sorry." Romans 6:16 explains that God gives us a choice. We can be slaves to sin which leads to death, or we can be slaves to obedience that leads to righteousness. The choice is ours.

ISAIAH 59:2

Because God is holy and sinless, he cannot be around sin. Our sin separates us from him. The only way the presence of God can live in us is through the forgiveness of our sins by the acceptance of Jesus Christ and his salvation. Although sin separates us from his presence, we are never separated from his unconditional love (Romans 8:38, 39).

SKETCHING THE DESIGN

LIAR, LIAR, PANTS ON FIRE!

Distribute a piece of blank paper and a writing utensil to each of your students. Have each person write down three truths and one lie about himself. Explain that the lie needs to be so convincing that it will fool those around them. As the game begins, they are to read each other's papers and try to guess which item on the list is a lie. Instruct them to be deceptive (with their truths) to make them sound like a lie. The person who is fooled by the lie has to initial the paper of the owner who wrote the lie. If the other person guesses the lie, then he just moves on to the next individual.

At the end of the game, determine who has the most initials. Consider giving an award to the biggest liar (the one with the most signatures) and to the best detective (the one with the least signatures).

Conclude this activity by asking:

- **Was it easy or hard to determine what was truth and what was the lie?**
- **When you realized what the truths were, did you always believe them?**
- **Why is it so hard to determine what is the truth?**

Comment, **"Listening through the world's ears, the voice of God and the voice of Satan seem to get mixed together. It is hard to determine what is the truth and what is the lie. This problem is not new. The Israelites' history is full of hearing problems. Today we will learn how the effects of sin humbled the Israelites to the point that they were ready and willing to follow God's truth to the tee."**

DON'T BREAK THE CIRCLE!

Choose two to three people to step out of the room. While they are outside, perform the following: Have one person stand in the middle of the room while the rest of the group makes a circle around him or her by interlocking their arms. Explain to the group that their job is to keep the outside person from getting to the person in the center of the circle.

Now ask the other people to come into the room. Tell them that their job is to get to the person in the center of the circle. The first one to reach the center person wins.

Afterward, ask the following:

- **What would have made it easier to get to the person in the middle?**
- **Who or what did the person in the middle represent?**
- **What did the outside people represent?**
- **What about the rest of the group?**
- **What separates us from God?**
- **What does Satan do to try to keep us from God?**
- **Does God want us to succeed at having a relationship with him?**

Comment, **"The Israelites' separation from God and Jerusalem was a result of their sin. Let's look in the book of Ezra to find out more about their return and their first stage in rebuilding."**

STUDYING THE BLUEPRINT

Materials needed:
Reproducible student sheet on page 22 of this book; writing utensils; Bibles

1 TRUTH OR DARE: PLAYING GAMES WITH GOD

Begin this activity by asking, **"Have you ever played the game 'Truth or Dare'? To play the game, one person spins a bottle. When the bottle stops, whomever it points to is asked a personal question. That person then has to answer the question truthfully or do a daring stunt. Most people today would much rather take a dare than face the truth of God's Word."**

Divide your students into four groups with each group answering one section of the *Truth or Dare* student sheet. When students are finished, ask them to share their answers, discussing them as time allows.

Close by saying, **"Knowing the truth of God's Word and not doing it is like 'playing chicken' with God. We continue to play—thinking that God will let his guard down, and we will get our way. The truth is that when we play games with God, he always wins. God lays the truth out before us in his Word. We know what he expects. It is our part to believe it, grabbing hold of it as if our lives depend on it—then live it."**

Check This . . .
While your students are working on their student sheets, play the song, "Lay It on the Line," by 4 Him, recorded on their album *The Message*.

Materials needed:
Reproducible student sheet on page 23 of this book; Bibles; writing utensils

2 HOUSE INSPECTION

Divide your students into two groups. Have each group read over the four scenarios found on their sheets. Assign one group the section that is marked "Good Foundation" and the other group the section marked "Bad Foundation." Begin by saying, **"Any builder will tell you that a house is only as good as its foundation. You are a house inspector; your job is to inspect houses. Look at these 'houses' and determine if there is a problem with the foundations. Circle the correct condition of the foundation. Then, look up the Scriptures and answer the questions pertaining to your type of foundation."**

Discuss the Scriptures, referring to the commentary as necessary.

REMODELING THE INTERIOR

Materials needed:
White construction paper; black bottled paint

1 TRUTH HURTS

Begin by saying, **"Sometimes the truth about us really hurts, but it is only when we see the truth and understand it that we can be changed. Psychologists use an 'Ink Blot' method to help reveal something about their patients' past in order to help them better understand themselves. Today we are going to use this method to reveal sin in our lives."**

Distribute the paper. Put a small glob of paint in the center of each paper. Have students very carefully fold the paper in half, sliding their hand across it gently to slightly crease. Next, have them open it carefully. Encourage them to share their discoveries. At first they might not take this activity seriously. They may comment that it looks like an alligator, a bird or a witch. You can bring the conversation around by saying, for instance, that the alligator can represent a sin in their life that is eventually going to gobble them up. The witch could represent someone in their life who is contributing to their sin.

You will be surprised at some of your students' expressions when God reveals to them that *he* knows their secret. Close by reading Isaiah 59:2. Then say, **"Our sin separates us from a holy God who wants to be near us. This week think about the sin that God just revealed to you. Think about how God sees that sin. Do you have the same desire to be close to him?"**

Check This . . .
Another option is to read a portion of the book *The Oath,* by Frank Peretti. This is a good fiction novel that deals with the issue of sin in a very horrifying way. On page 386 of the book is a copy of the creed upon which the people in the story founded their town. Read the creed and ask, **"How do people in real life make 'reason' their God? Why would people believe the statement, 'Only by reason can truth be established'? Why would people choose to serve sin?"**

2 SELF-INSPECTION

Close this session by asking these questions:

- **In inspecting your own temple, how is your foundation?**
- **Is it firm and steady? Or is it cracking?**
- **Is your foundation built on truth?**
- **In evaluating your temple and the sin in your life, what do you need to be in "move-in condition" to house the living God: a good sterile cleaning, a total overhaul—a demolition crew?**

Give students a few minutes to evaluate themselves. Then read Isaiah 59:2. Conclude by saying, **"This verse says that because of our sin God had to cover his face; we caused a separation that leads to a spiritual death. Although this is a hard truth to swallow, the Bible also promises that we cannot be separated from God's love. He has a desire to have a relationship with us. Can you picture him with tears in his eyes when he longs to be close to us but cannot? Do what it takes to have a relationship with him. Pick up a hammer and a saw and start building your temple now. God is worth it."**

Close by asking God to guide each "temple" to be a living sanctuary to house the presence of God. Distribute copies of **The Midweek Clean** to your students.

TRUTH OR DARE

TRUTH

In what ways does Romans 1:20-32 explain the **truth** about the fall of the Israelites? (Refer to 2 Chronicles 36:14-23 if necessary.)

How does this compare to mankind today?

In Ezra 3:1-6 circle the words "accordance," "required," "prescribed" and "appointed" in your Bibles. To build their temple, what **truth** were the Israelites following?

How is this different from their actions before their captivity?

Believing in God's **truth** and his ability to take care of them, what did the Israelites finish building next? (Ezra 3:7-13)

What was their reaction to this accomplishment? (vv. 10-13)

What foundation of **truth** is our temple built on? (1 Corinthians 3:10, 11) How solid is this foundation? (2 Timothy 2:19)

DARE

What did mankind **dare** to do? (Romans 1:21-23) What did they exchange the **truth** for? (v. 25)

Did mankind know what the **truth** was?

Do we have any excuse for sin? (v. 20)

What did God do about mankind's (and the Israelites') sin? (vv. 24, 26, 28)

What did the Israelites **dare** to build despite their fears? (Ezra 3:2, 3) Who or what did they fear and why would an altar help?

Since the Israelites **dared** to return to Jerusalem to do something God wanted them to do; and they **dared** to praise God, crediting him for this accomplishment, who took notice from far away? (Ezra 3:13)

By whose standards do most people **dare** to attempt to build upon God's foundation? (1 Corinthians 3:18, 19) What happens to their *house* when they attempt this? (3:12-17)

The truth about yourself—do you dare to find out?

How is sinning like playing games with God?

Do you ever try to play?

Dare to be different—just love God back!

HOUSE INSPECTION

HOUSE #1

Jim is a 17-year-old Christian. He has been in church most of his life and is faithful in attending youth group and church. Overall, he is a pretty good guy. One of Jim's favorite things to do is to go to movies or rent them. He doesn't see anything wrong with watching R-rated movies. He says he is able to determine what is bad and what is not; therefore the movies do not bother his relationship with Christ.

Foundation Good
Foundation Bad

HOUSE #2

Elise is pretty, smart and well-liked by most. Her parents go to church, and she believes in God without a doubt. She is involved in drama club and choir at school and tries hard to make straight A's. She is kind and volunteers frequently at the local day care. When asked why she is not active in church, Elise says, "My life is great now. Why would I want to change anything? My life is so busy, I don't have time to volunteer at church or go to youth group. God will understand if I wait until I'm an adult to get involved in church. Besides, I'm not a bad person, so what's to judge me on anyway?"

Foundation Good
Foundation Bad

HOUSE #3

Gary is a people person. He likes people and needs them around him. He believes that God loves everyone. He prides himself on being a peacemaker. He has a hard time understanding why people are so judgmental. He says, "How can people be so homophobic or get so angry about the abortion issue? I may not live that way but what might not be right for me might be all right for others—to each his own. We just need to mind our own business and give people the right to live how they want. Jesus was not a judgmental person, so why do we need to be?"

Foundation Good
Foundation Bad

HOUSE #4

Jennifer is 16 years old. She has been dating John for six months now. They go everywhere together—to ball games, the movies, to church and youth group. She could not believe she could have such a close relationship with such a nice guy. The other night they got a little too close. Her mom and dad were gone and she invited John over to swim. They started to kiss and then things got a little heavy. Jennifer feels awful about the whole thing. The next day she went to a lady she trusted at the church to tell her what had happened and ask for help. She apologized to John for inviting him over and made a commitment to never be alone again.

Foundation Good   Foundation Bad

GOOD FOUNDATION

What did the Israelites build first despite their fears? Why did they build this first? (Ezra 3:1-6)

In what condition should a spiritual foundation be? (2 Timothy 2:19)

Circle the words "accordance," "required," "prescribed" and "appointed" in your Bible. What guidelines were the Israelites trying to follow closely in their building? (Ezra 3:1-6)

What foundation has already been laid for us? At what expense was it laid? (1 Corinthians 3:10, 11)

What did the Israelites rejoice over when it was finished? Why was this so important to them? Why did some cry? (Ezra 3:7-13)

What will happen if we build on it with faulty materials? With good materials? (1 Corinthians 3:12-15)

BAD FOUNDATION

Name the qualities of a bad foundation found in Romans 1:20-32. What deserves death? (v. 32) Did the Israelites ever possess these qualities? What was the result? (Refer to 2 Chronicles 36:14-23.)

The Midweek Clean
A Guide for Remodeling the Interior

Something to Read

Something to Read

Take a few moments to reread Ezra 3:11-13.

Something to Think About

Rebuilding the foundation of the temple was a joyous occasion. Most of the people rejoiced, but there were those who wept, possibly the older people, because they remembered the old temple and how glorious it was.

Do you think that the beauty of the temple was important to God? What is important to God when it comes to our *temple?* (1 Samuel 16:7)

Why do people spend so much time and money on the outside of their *temple* but fail to do anything about the inside? Those who remembered the old temple might have let the memories of it distract their focus on what was material rather than spiritual.

Is there anything that is distracting you from focusing on and building upon your relationship with God?

Something to Do

Other than God, write down the top three things that are the most important to you. Be honest.

1. _____
2. _____
3. _____

Would you cry if they were gone? Beside each item write down how much time and money you spend on these things. (Write down the hourly/weekly amount.) Now write three reasons why God is important to you.

1. _____
2. _____
3. _____

How much time and money do you give to him? (Write down the hourly/weekly amount.) Compare the two lists. Where is most of your focus? Take the first list and tear it into pieces, symbolizing its importance compared to God. Put the second list someplace where you will see it continually as a reminder of who is first in your life.

". . . and all the people gave a great shout of praise to the LORD, because the foundation of the house of the LORD was laid." Ezra 3:11

HURLING THE ROBBLE

LAYING THE FOUNDATION

EZRA 4

Just when they thought life was going pretty good, the Israelites began to experience major opposition. The people who lived in the lands around Jerusalem saw how well things were going and did not like it (see also Ezra 3:3). These were the mixed race of people later known as Samaritans (2 Kings 17:33). The Samaritans did not want this once strong and powerful nation to become powerful again.

Round 1—It's a fight of the century, a match between Israel and the Samaritans. They had a long history of hate. Israel and "Sam" enter the boxing ring to duke it out. The enemy's first approach was very subtle. They were nice. They offered to help build the temple because they said they too worshiped this God. They failed to mention that they worshiped a whole lot of other gods too. Red flag! Old Zerubbabel probably thought, "Been there, done that!" The Israelites refused, knowing that compromising their beliefs is what got them in this mess in the first place. Ding! Israel wins round one. Satan must have thought this sin worked once, so let's try it again. He never gives up!

Round 2— Sam comes out of his corner putting forth some devastating blows. First he discouraged the Israelites by making them afraid. Ouch! (v. 4) Then he hired royal counselors to intimidate the Israelites and "frustrate their plans." Ooff! Then the bunch of wimps wrote letters to two Persian kings accusing them falsely. Don't you hate it when you try to do something good and people lie about you? You cannot change the thoughts and attitudes of others. That is up to them. All you can do is live your life above reproach and trust God to deal with the hearts of people.

In the letter, the enemies wrote about their past history, using words like *troublesome* and *rebellious*. Verse 15 states, "That is why this city was destroyed." The hard part was it was all true. Could you imagine all your mistakes written on paper and stored in a library (vv. 15, 19)? Satan is good at punching us where it really hurts. He knows our past like the back of his hand, and he will never let us forget it.

The Israelites experienced 80 years of nonstop opposition. (Note

LESSON TEXT
Ezra 4:1–6:15

LESSON FOCUS
"Then the peoples around them set out to discourage the people of Judah and make them afraid to go on building." (Ezra 4:4)

LESSON GOALS
As a result of participating in this lesson, students will:

- Learn about the obstacles that hindered the Israelites from getting the temple rebuilt.
- Understand that continuing in sin slows them down or stops their spiritual growth.
- Discover how, with God's help, they can be successful in throwing off the problems that keep them from accomplishing his work.
- Realize that Christians should expect trials, but God provides a solution to each problem they face, as he did for the Israelites.

that chapter four is not in chronological order; vv. 6, 7 mention Kings Xerxes and Artaxerxes, who were kings after Darius—see v. 24.) The enemy's fighting techniques worked so well that six years after the Israelites started the temple, the work on it stopped (v. 24). Right hook . . . Israel down for the count.

EZRA 5

The worked stopped for 16 years—no doubt their enemies loved this! During this time, the Israelites built their own beautiful houses and settled down, raised their kids, maybe even sat relaxing in the sun while sipping lemonade. Then along came Haggai and Zechariah, prophets of God! Haggai preached a humdinger of a sermon and Zechariah told a series of cool visions (as recorded in the books of Haggai and Zechariah). As a result of this, the Israelites got off their tails and returned to work. Change always happens when God's Word is revealed and taken to heart. The count: 8, 9 . . . Israel gets up and goes to his corner. Haggai gives him a drink, and Zechariah rubs his shoulders. Hey! Who is that big guy standing over them?

Round 3—Ding! It is a fight to the finish. A new Persian official named Tattenai takes it upon himself to check things out by asking for proof of authorization for their building contract. That was probably brought on by the continuous complaints from the neighbors. He then writes a letter reporting to King Darius the progress of the construction of the temple.

EZRA 6:1-15

Wait a minute. Someone else is getting in the ring and fighting for Israel. Boy, is he big! Those hands look like they could move a mountain! King Darius issued an order for the archives of Babylon to be searched. And the answer to Israel's problems was found in a pagan library. King Darius then issued a decree of his own (vv. 6-12). It said: 1) No one was to interfere with the building of the temple. 2) He commanded the Jews to work. 3) Their enemies were not only supposed to leave them alone, but also had to pay for the work to be done. They even had to provide whatever was needed for the sacrifices. Sweet justice! 4) If anyone interfered, his house was to be destroyed, and he was to be hung on one of its beams.

The temple was completed according to the command of God and the kings of Persia (vv. 14, 15). The Samaritans are down for the count: 8, 9, 10. God wins!

EZRA 6:16-22

Victory celebration! There was no weeping this time. The Israelites' goal was "to seek the LORD" and to honor him for "changing the attitude of the king of Assyria." A deliverance from God easily displays our lack of ability to handle our own problems. Lesson learned? Don't underestimate God's power to overcome obstacles and enemies in your life!

1 JOHN 3:6, 9, 10

There is a difference between struggling with sin and continuing in sin. The difference is in our attitude toward it and whether or not we take God at his Word. This Scripture tells us that it is wrong to continue in sin when we know it is against God. Everyone sins, but the one "born of God" will not become indifferent toward it—he will have the desire to stop.

HEBREWS 12:1-4

Sin makes a tangled mess of our lives. These verses say to throw it off so that it does not slow us down in our Christian walk. Even Jesus was faced with opposition from men. That's why he understands our struggles (see Hebrews 4:15, 16). When we keep our eyes on him, we will not grow weary.

2 TIMOTHY 3:12-14

If you are following Christ as closely as possible, expect opposition from Satan. There are no exceptions. Satan doesn't bother with those that he already has; he wants what belongs to God. Unbelief sees obstacles; faith sees opportunities. When opposition comes, "continue" in the Word and stand on it.

SKETCHING THE DESIGN

1 KNOTS AND TANGLES

Divide your students into two to four groups. Have the groups clump together facing outward. Choose someone to help you as you tangle, weave and tie the group together (do not tie above the shoulders or around the ankles). Have each group complete an obstacle course going over, around and under obstacles, in their tangled mess. This can be accomplished as a race or by timing each individual group. To make it a little harder, give them objects that they have to hold onto, as a group, while they complete the race. Conclude this activity by asking:

- **How hard was it to complete the obstacle course?**
- **Would it have been easier if you had not been tangled?**
- **What are some things that entangle us—causing us to stumble in our walk with Christ?**

Comment, **"It is frustrating trying to follow God when the obstacles in our path slow us down or cause us to go in the wrong direction. It seems easier if we could just give up. The book of Ezra describes the obstacles the Israelites experienced while they were working on the temple. Let's take a look."**

Materials needed:
Two to four 20-foot-long pieces of soft nylon rope or heavy string; hard-to-hold-onto objects such as large beach balls; a mini-obstacle course

Check This . . .
"Knots" is a simple game with no props. Each person should stand facing another person. They are to reach out and grab hands of the person across from them as if shaking hands. Then they are to untangle themselves, making one large circle while still holding hands. For complete instructions on this game, see pp.117, 118 of the book *Silver Bullets*, by Karl Rohnke (Project Adventure).

Materials needed:
A backpack full of different sizes and colors of rocks

2 ALL I GOT WAS THIS BAG OF ROCKS!

Begin by saying, **"I brought a very special collection with me today. But since I cannot teach and wear this at the same time, I would like someone to volunteer to wear it for me."** Choose a volunteer to put on the backpack. Then have him sit down. Comment, **"Oh, I almost forgot. I am trying hard not to make this collection more important than God. Could you please stand up and sit down every time I say the word _God_ or _Jesus_?"** After awhile, if you see this is going to become a distraction, and you have made your point, have the student just sit down quietly.

STUDYING THE BLUEPRINT

Materials needed:
Reproducible student sheet on page 30 of this book; Bibles; writing utensils

1 THE JERUSALEM DAILY REPORTER

Begin this activity by saying, **"Do you ever feel that life can be unfair? You try so hard to walk the Christian walk and just when life is good, something bad happens. It is like being in one continual boxing match. The Israelites' experience was the same. They laid the foundation of the temple, making sure they did everything according to God's Word. Then, they began to build the temple. They were hit with one obstacle after another. Let's take a look at what those obstacles were."**

Divide students into five groups, distributing copies of the student sheet to each group. Instruct each group to read its portion of the Scripture and then write a story under its headline as if it were appearing in an edition of _The Jerusalem Daily Reporter._

After groups have completed their work, allow a spokesperson from each group to read their articles. Comment as necessary, referring to the Scripture commentary for background information.

Materials needed:
Reproducible student sheet on page 31 of this book; Bibles; writing utensils

2 HAVE A NICE TRIP— SEE YOU NEXT FALL

Say something like this: **"Satan is like a recurring nightmare that just won't go away. He is constantly trying every technique to trip us up and slow us down in building our lives as a temple of God. Check out these techniques that Satan used on the Israelites; then compare them with his tactics today."**

Pass out writing utensils and copies of the student sheet. Let students work individually or in groups of two.

REMODELING THE INTERIOR

1 GOD THE AVENGER!

Form a large circle. Ask, **"Is there an obstacle in your life that is keeping you from growing closer to God? Maybe you are just having a tough time and you are angry at God for allowing you to go through it. We don't always know why bad things happen. However, we *do* know that God cares about us; and he is bigger than any obstacle that comes in our path. He is faithful to stand by us and help us through. The greatest part is that God can take any situation and make good come out of it. Unbelief sees obstacles; faith sees opportunities. Take a moment and think of the biggest obstacle in your life. Reflect on it as I read Psalm 18:1-19. Compare that obstacle to God and you may see that it is not so big."**

Close by reading Psalm 18:1-19 and thanking God for taking care of his temple.

2 LAY YOUR BURDENS DOWN!

Ask the person that has been carrying the backpack to come forward. Say, **"I want to thank _____ for taking care of my backpack for me. Have you figured out what my precious cargo is? Rocks!"** Pull out some of the rocks. **"These rocks are all different sizes, shapes and colors. Some of them are very old and some are new. I have had them for so long it is hard to let go of them."**

Ask the volunteer, **"How hard was it to carry these rocks? Were you able to concentrate on the lesson?"** Ask students, **"What do these rocks symbolize in the Christian life? They may represent circumstances in your life that are weighing you down. They could be habits, possessions or people in our lives that, no matter how bad or how heavy they become, we refuse to let go. As Christians, we need to trust God with every aspect of our lives.** (Read 1 Corinthians 10:13.) **This verse states that God is faithful and provides a way out so we can stand firm. Whatever obstacle is slowing you down, 'let go and let God.'"**

Conclude by thanking God for being faithful to take care of his temple. Distribute copies of **The Midweek Clean** to your students.

Check This . . .
You may want to end this session with the song "Hope to Carry On," by Caedmon's Call, recorded on their self-titled debut album.

Check This . . .
An effective way to combat Satan is to memorize Scripture, then quote it to him when he plagues you. (It worked for Jesus in the desert.)

Have students memorize 1 Corinthians 10:13, using this method: 1) Read the verse a couple of times. 2) Toss one person a ball and have him say the first word of the verse. 3) That person tosses the ball to the next person, who will quote the next word. 4) Toss the ball back and forth until the verse is completed.

THE JERUSALEM DAILY REPORTER

Inside story: The Samaritans were long-time enemies of the Israelites. They were not happy that the Israelites were making a comeback, so they decided they were going to do whatever it took to stop them from building the temple. You are an investigative reporter. Seek out information and write your story under each headline.

Same-Song Sam Claims Godliness— Israel Denies
Read Ezra 4:1-3.

Intimidation Is Sam's Game; Israel Is Down for the Count
Read Ezra 4:4, 5.

Israel Accused Falsely . . . or Were They?
Read Ezra 4:6-23.

Governor Demands Proof— Israel Continues to Work
Read Ezra 5:1–6:15.

Israeli Descendant Claims Perfection Yet Sympathizes with Gentile Youths
Read Hebrews 4:15, 16; 12:1-4; 2 Timothy 3:12-14.

HAVE A NICE TRIP— SEE YOU NEXT FALL

#1
Have you ever had someone be nice to you only to harm you because he had an ulterior motive? How did you handle it?
Read Ezra 4:1-4. Who was being nice to the Israelites? Were they sincere? What did they want the Israelites to stop doing?

#2
Have you ever had someone intimidate you so much that you compromised your beliefs or stopped doing something you knew was right? How did you handle it? Was there anyone there to help you?
Read Ezra 4:4, 5. What did their enemies do to stop the work on the temple?
What eventually happened as a result of this? (4:24) Name two people (and their jobs) who motivated the Israelites to rebuild again. (5:1, 2)

#3
Have you ever had anyone lie about you or falsely accuse you? How did it make you feel? How did you react? Have you ever been reminded of your past, only to have it bring you down or halt you in your Christian walk?
Read Ezra 4:6-23. Who wrote a letter and to whom did he write it?
What false information was given in the letter? (vv. 12-16) According to the account in 2 Chronicles 36:11-13, 17, what was true in the letter? (vv. 15, 19) What happened as a result of this letter? (v. 24)

#4
Read Ezra 5:1–6:15.
At this point, the rebuilding of the temple had come to a standstill for 16 years. God sent two prophets to encourage the Israelites to work again.
What governor came snooping around the building site? (5:6) What information did he report to the king? (vv. 7-16) (Perhaps a better name for him would be "Tattletale.")
What did the king do with the information? (6:1-3, 6, 7)
What happened as result of the king's edict? (6:14)

#5
According to Hebrews 4:15, 16 and 12:1-4 , what Israelite descendant also had struggles and opposition? How does this knowledge help you in your struggles?
According to 2 Timothy 3:12-14, is it normal for Christians to experience hard times and struggles? How are we to handle them when they come?

The Midweek Clean
A Guide for Remodeling the Interior

Something to Read

Something to Read

Take a few moments to reread Ezra 5:17–6:12, 22.

Something to Think About

Whose attitude was changed in these verses? What kind of attitude did this person start out with? What or who changed his attitude? According to the dictionary, an attitude is a manner or a feeling. Can we actually change the thoughts and attitudes of others? Read Hebrews 4:12, 13. Who judges the thoughts and attitudes of man? Is anything hidden from God? Can you think of one person who dislikes you unjustly? Can you change the way that person perceives you? Who can change that person's attitude? Do you believe that God can help you with people problems?

Something to Do

The best way to win a battle is to know who your enemy is. Ephesians 6 says we are not in a fight with people, but with Satan. Think of a person who has given you a hard time or has become an obstacle in your Christian life. Each time you see that person, ask yourself, "How would Jesus see this person? How would he treat this person?" As hard as it may be, pray for that person every day this week. What can you do for that person to show him or her that God has taken control of this area of your life? Do it!

"For seven days they celebrated with joy . . . because the LORD had filled them with joy by changing the attitude of the king of Assyria, so that he assisted them in the work on the house of God, the God of Israel." Ezra 6:22

WHO'S IN CHARGE HERE?

LAYING THE FOUNDATION

EZRA 7:1–8:36

There is a 60-year gap between Ezra 6 and Ezra 7. Zerubbabel, Jeshua, Haggai and Zechariah, key people in building the temple, were probably dead. In these verses, Ezra, a descendant of Aaron, the brother of Moses, was commissioned by God to go to Jerusalem. Although he grew up in Babylon, a polytheistic (believing in many gods) nation, Ezra still knew God's Word, dedicating himself to living and teaching it. He must have been a highly respected man in the royal palace for he was able to approach King Artaxerxes and his court (v. 14) to ask permission to leave Babylon to go to Jerusalem. The king not only granted him permission, but he issued a decree allowing any Jew in Babylon to go (v. 14). The king of Persia gave Ezra money and supplies for the temple. He also made Ezra an authority figure in Jerusalem to make sure the people of that city knew and obeyed the law of God (vv. 25, 26).

It sounded like the kings of Persia were pretty nice people, helping out the Israelites all the time. But, by reading the book of Esther (which also takes place between Ezra 6 and 7) you discover how King Artaxerxes' father was going to "kill and annihilate all the Jews" (Esther 3:13). Approaching the king was no picnic in the park. Ezra had to have been a person of integrity and courage to influence a pagan king in such a way. The king was aware of the power of the one true God but not enough to worship him. His motive was to stay away from God's wrath (7:23). Notice how many times the phrase "the hand of God" is mentioned. Ezra realized the sovereignty of God and his power over any other king. Ezra accomplished great things not by what he knew or who he knew, but by recognizing who was in charge—God.

Four months later (7:8, 9), a group of 1,514 men (8:1-20) plus families arrived at Jerusalem praising God for a safe journey. Throughout these two chapters, we see God raising up a godly, courageous leader in a godless nation to do an incredible task in leading others home (Ezra 7:28). Sounds like a good reason to teach youth as well!

LESSON TEXT
Ezra 7:1–8:36

LESSON FOCUS
". . . Because the hand of the LORD my God was on me, I took courage and gathered leading men from Israel to go up with me." Ezra 7:28

LESSON GOALS
As a result of participating in this lesson, students will:

- Learn that God provided godly people—Zerubbabel, Jeshua, Haggai, Zechariah and Ezra—to help the Israelites when they needed it the most.
- Understand that God provides people to help us live the Christian life to the fullest.
- Discover that it takes courage to give God full ownership of our lives and serve him in an ungodly world.
- Realize that God is more than qualified to build our temple; our job is to trust and obey him as master of our lives.

HEBREWS 3:3-6, 12

God is the builder of everything, and he has greater honor than us, his house. We do not have to put God in the place of honor. He is already there, but all the better for us if we recognize his dominion over us. *The Life Application Bible* states about this verse, "We are not saved by being steadfast and firm in our faith, but our courage and hope do reveal that our faith is real."[1] It takes courage to be a Christian, a holy dwelling where God's presence lives. Is our faith real? Do we have the courage to not turn away from the living God?

ZECHARIAH 4:6-9

This is a message God sent through the prophet Zechariah to encourage Zerubbabel. God said that the temple would be completed through the leadership of Zerubbabel, but God would be the power source through which it would be accomplished. He also empowers us to build our lives.

ZECHARIAH 6:12, 13, 15

This is a prophecy about Christ (the Branch). He will build our temple and take his place on the throne. God requires obedience and commitment to the building of our temple (v. 15). When we live in whole-hearted obedience (not perfection), God blesses us with people in our lives to help us build.

SKETCHING THE DESIGN

1 THE PAGEMASTER

The Pagemaster is a partially-animated movie about a young boy named Richard Tyler, who is afraid of everything. Due to a storm, he takes refuge in a library where he becomes an illustration of a book. This is where he meets the Pagemaster, who gives Richard three tests he must face before he can go home. All Richard desires is to find the exit, but the Pagemaster wants Richard to grow "to incredible heights." During his adventure he meets three friends who help him through each test. This movie represents God's mastery over our lives and how he provides people to help us in our Christian lives. Often, all we want out of life is to make it through, but God's desire is for us to grow. The entire movie is full of incredible parallels.

Since time is limited, begin the movie where Richard becomes an illustration and meets the Pagemaster. End where Richard runs into the telephone booth. If time allows, fast-forward to the end of the movie or have a second video cued up. Begin where he meets the Pagemaster again. Stop the video where he enters the exit sign to go home.

Afterward, discuss the movie by asking:

• **What was Richard's goal from the beginning of his adventure?**

Materials needed:
VCR; TV; *The Pagemaster* video, by Twentieth Century Fox

Check This . . .
Show a clip of the television sitcom *Home Improvement.* Try to choose an episode in which Tim is remodeling a home. Use this as an example of how we think we are experts on how to run our own life; but there is only one expert, God.

- **What was the Pagemaster's goal for Richard?**
- **Was there more than one way to get to the exit?**
- **Who knew the best way?**
- **In Richard's adventure, where was he told to look when he was in doubt?**
- **Do you ever feel like Richard Tyler, wanting the easy way through the Christian life because it is too hard or too scary?**
- **Who is the Pagemaster of your life?**

Ask, **"Today we're going to look at the Pagemaster of your life."**

Check This . . .
Another suggestion is to show a clip of the movie *The Money Pit* (MCA Home video), featuring Tom Hanks. This movie does not depict the greatest of morals. Show a short clip to illustrate how we invest so much in ourselves. However, without a good contractor, God, and his investment, Jesus, our attempts at remodeling are destructive.

2 CONTRACTING WITH THE CONTRACTOR

Ask a contractor to come in and briefly describe his or her occupation to your students. Allow time for them to ask questions. If a contractor is not available, approach a contracting company. Ask them to give you a description of what their company does and how a person would go about choosing a contractor.

Ask your students the following:

- **What if a person with no knowledge of construction decided to contract his own house and build it on his own without any help?**
- **What would the end result of his house be?**
- **Would it be built correctly?**
- **What does a subcontractor do?** *(A subcontractor is a person qualified in a certain aspect of building, who is hired by the contractor to build that particular area of the house.)*

Comment, **"Today, we are going to discover the qualifications of the contractor of our house and who he has subcontracted to help us in our building."**

STUDYING THE BLUEPRINT

1 GOOD HELP IS HARD TO FIND

Distribute writing utensils and copies of the reproducible student sheet. After you have allowed students enough time to work, discuss the questions, referring to the commentary as needed.

Comment, **"When we give God complete mastery over our lives, he provides incredible resources to help in our walk with him. God is not a big meanie with his arms crossed and a scowl on his face, watching us humans flounder around on earth suffering. Have you ever seen a fish out of water? It flips and flops, unable to go anywhere until it dies of exhaustion. God provides his Word, people, good advice, the Holy Spirit and uplifting music to help us become the best building we can be for him. He not only builds the house; he provides the materials. So often we try to**

Materials needed:
Reproducible student sheet on page 38 of this book; Bibles; writing utensils

take control of our lives or entrust them to someone unqualified. The results are often messy. Our job is not to hammer away aimlessly. Rather, it is to trust and obey the one with the power to complete our house to perfection. Can you trust the one who is more qualified than any other to build your house?"

2 GOD FOR HIRE!

Begin this activity by saying, **"If you were going to contract your house out to someone, what qualifications would you look for in that person?"** As students respond, write the qualifications on a piece of newsprint.

Read Hebrews 3:3-6 and ask, **"According to these verses, who is the builder/contractor of our house?"** Divide students into four groups. Distribute copies of the student sheet and have each group complete the work, writing down the qualities of God that make him qualified to be the contractor of our house. When they have completed the worksheet, have them each read their portion of the Scripture and their results.

Discuss by saying, **"God is more than qualified to do anything he wants to do, but he chooses to spend his time on us because he loves us and wants to have a relationship with us. As the contractor of his house, he provides us with subcontractors to help us in our building."**

Read the following verses with your students to determine who helped God; what they did; and the end result (Ezra 5:1; 6:14, 22/*Haggai and Zechariah*; Ezra 5:2 and Zechariah 4:6-9/*Jeshua and Zerubbabel*; Ezra 7:6-11; 21-27/ *Ezra*; Ezra 8:15-19, 24/*capable men*). Conclude by asking, **"Who in your life has God provided to help you?"**

Materials needed:
Reproducible student sheet on page 39 of this book; Bibles; newsprint; magic marker; writing utensils

Check This . . .
A song you might play as they are working on their student sheets is "It's All in Who You Know," by the Newsboys, recorded on their album *Take Me to Your Leader.*

REMODELING THE INTERIOR

1 ONE MILLION REASONS TO TRUST GOD

Play the song "One Million Reasons to Trust You," by Aaron Jeoffrey, recorded on his album of the same title. On the chalkboard, write down reasons why we should trust God. Say, **"So many times instead of trusting God with our life we just get angry with him for the circumstances we experience. We do not always know why God allows us to experience some of the things we do in life. But one thing we *do* know—he is worth trusting. He can take any circumstance and make something wonderful come from it. Ask yourself, 'Is God in control of my life?'"**

Have a circle prayer, thanking God for all the reasons he gives us to trust him.

Materials needed:
CD or tape player; the song "One Million Reasons to Trust You," by Aaron Jeoffrey; chalk and chalkboard

2 SIGN ON THE DOTTED LINE

Pass out the paper and writing utensils. Ask your students to write down reasons why they are qualified to run their own lives. Tell them to be honest. Then have them compare their list with the qualities of God as laid out in Isaiah 40:10-31. Ask, "**Who is more qualified to build and own our house? In comparing our abilities to God's, we realize how unqualified we really are.**" Play the song "I Surrender All," by Clay Crosse. Close with prayer. Distribute copies of **The Midweek Clean** to your students.

Materials needed:
Paper; writing utensils; Bibles; the song "I Surrender All," by Clay Crosse, recorded on his album, *My Place is With You*; CD or tape player

Check This . . .
Another option is to have your students draw themselves as a house, as God would see them spiritually. Have them color in the sections that God owns.

GOOD HELP IS HARD TO FIND

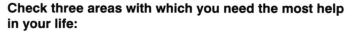

Check three areas with which you need the most help in your life:

financial   friendships   boy/girl relationship

parents/family   stress   grades/school

Christianity   dealing with a past experience

living in general

To whom would you most likely go to ask for help? (Circle one.)

parents   friends   youth minister   teacher   counselor

What main quality do you look for in a person to help you?

good-looking   intelligent   good listener   compassionate   a devoted Christian   wise

Circle the answer that best describes your relationship with God right now:

Judge/offender   Master/puppy dog   Lion/victim   best friends   Father/child

no relationship

When we follow God closely, he is faithful in sending people to help us. Read the verses below and discover who helped the Israelites.

VERSES	PERSON(S)	WHAT WAS THEIR OCCUPATION(S)?	HOW DID THEY HELP?	WHO GOT THE CREDIT?
Ezra 5:1; 6:14, 22				
Ezra 5:2; Zechariah 4:6-9				
Ezra 7:6-11, 21-27				
Ezra 8:15-19, 24				

Who actually builds our temple? (Zechariah 6:12, 13, 15; Hebrews 3:3-6)

Who holds the highest honor in our temple?

GOD FOR HIRE

You want to hire someone to design, contract and build your house for you. First, you want to check out his qualifications to make sure he is able to do the job and do it well.

Application for Employment

Name: God, Jehovah, Yahweh (too many to list)

Address: Heaven and hearts of men

Past and current employment: Creator of the universe, Earth and man; Savior of the world; Lover of the souls of man; Counselor; Guide; Friend; Father (too many to list)

References: Creation, Adam, Noah, Jonah, Moses, Ezra, Peter, Paul (too many to list)

Qualifications:

Isaiah 40:6-11

Isaiah 40:12-17

Isaiah 40:18-24

Isaiah 40:25-31

The Midweek Clean
A Guide for Remodeling the Interior

Something to Read

Reread Ezra 7:1–8:36.

Something to Think About

Underline the six times that the phrase, "the hand of God" or "the hand of the Lord" is mentioned.

On whom was the hand of God?

What was accomplished because of the hand of God?

How did Ezra know it was the hand of God and not just a matter of coincidence?

Look at Ezra 7:10, 14. What was in Ezra's hand? Would this contribute to why he knew so much about what God was doing? Explain.

What did the king command Ezra to do with "the wisdom" of his God? (7:25, 26)

Something to Do

Put your hand on a piece of white paper and trace around it. Carry it with you for 24 hours. On each finger, write an event or a thought that God used to guide you during that day. At the end of the day, take time to thank him for guiding you in each of those ways.

"'. . . The gracious hand of our God is on everyone who looks to him, but his great anger is against all who forsake him.'" Ezra 8:22

SET IN STONE

LAYING THE FOUNDATION

EZRA 8:35–9:2

The second group of exiles, under the leadership of Ezra, returned from captivity to Jerusalem. The first group of exiles had already been in Jerusalem for 80 years. Ezra returned to find the temple rebuilt, but the peoples' hearts and lives were still in need of repair. Ezra, who had devoted himself to the study and observance of God's Word (7:10, 25, 26), became a great spiritual leader among the Israelites. Again God provided someone at just the right time to lead the Israelites to a restored relationship with him.

EZRA 9:3-15

Ezra was appalled that the Israelites would give into this age-old sin. Marrying pagan women and worshiping their idols was direct disobedience against God's law. Ezra reacted to sin like every Christian should react. The closer we get to the light, the more clearly we see the dirt in our house. Ezra knew Israel's sin because he was close to the light (God) through prayer and Bible study. His reaction also reminds us of Christ's reaction to our sin. He took it as his own. He mourned over it and even called out to God on the cross.

EZRA 10

With Ezra's example, the people of Israel began mourning and weeping over their sin, realizing how far from God they had come (vv. 1-3). They *recognized* their sin. They *realized* it was wrong and it was punishable. They *reacted* to it by mourning over it and confessing it (vv. 1, 11). They *rid* themselves of what was separating them from God (v. 17). They *replaced* it with a promise to God and God's promise to them of the Messiah (Zechariah 9). The end result was a *restored relationship* with God. It does not matter how far we wander away from God; he always welcomes us back with open arms.

ROMANS 3:23-26

God did not *react* to our sin by giving us what we deserved—death

LESSON TEXT
Ezra 8:35–10:4

LESSON FOCUS
". . . But in spite of this, there is still hope for Israel. Now let us make a covenant before our God . . ."
(Ezra 10:2, 3)

LESSON GOALS
• As a result of participating in this lesson, students will:
• Discover that the Israelites mourned over their sin, confessed their sins to God and offered sacrifices for them.
• Recognize that Christ is the ultimate sacrifice for our sins.
• Believe that God has promised to forgive our sins and remember them no more when we commit ourselves to him.
• Release their sins in a special ceremony as an act of covenant between them and God.

(Romans 6:23). Rather, he *acted* in behalf of our sin by sending his Son as the ultimate sacrifice. Although we deserve death and punishment, we are justified (**just** as **if I'd** never sinned) freely through the blood of Christ. Why? He loves us and wants us close to him (restoration). What Christ did on the cross was not a reaction—it was an *act* of love.

SKETCHING THE DESIGN

1 ACT OR REACT

Materials needed:
Newspapers; scissors; writing utensils; scrap paper

Distribute newspapers, making sure that each student has several sheets. Then, ask them to find an article that causes an emotional reaction in them. Have them tear or cut it out, writing on their paper a response to these questions:

- **What was your reaction to this article?**
- **What emotion did it cause? Why?**
- **If you were God, how would you react to this situation?**

Then discuss the articles with your students by saying: **"Sometimes when I read the paper or watch TV and I see what is going on in the world, I wonder how God feels about each situation. If I were God, I know how I would react—a lightning bolt from the sky. That would straighten up those sinners! But fortunately God is not that hasty. In this lesson we will learn from the Israelites' reaction to their own sin and how God responds to ours."**

2 GRAND CANYON

Materials needed:
Decorations such as lamp stand, mats or carpet squares; curtain; candles; large bowl with water; towel; CD or tape player; the song "Grand Canyon," by Susan Ashton, recorded on her album *So Far*

Ahead of time, decorate your meeting room to look like a temple. Take all the chairs out and put down mats or carpet squares. String a curtain across the room to represent the Holy of Holies. Borrow a candelabra like those used in weddings, and light some candles. Turn off the lights. As the students enter, have them take off their shoes and wash their hands. Play the song "Grand Canyon," by Susan Ashton, as they quietly find their places.

Say something like, **"If you were an Israelite and you wanted forgiveness for your sins, you would have to enter the temple to offer sacrifices for your sins. Although you could enter the temple, you could not enter into God's presence. Only one man could be in the presence of God. The High Priest was allowed to go into the curtained room called the 'Holy of Holies' once a year on behalf of all the Israelites. Could you imagine never being in the presence of God? Sin separates us from God. Just as the song we just played says, there is a canyon between us and God. The Israelites offered sacrifices to deal with their sin. In this lesson we will find out how to bridge the canyon and how God deals with our sin."**

Check This . . .
The Source, by Scott Dyer and Nancy Beach (Zondervan) is an excellent resource to have on hand when planning lessons. It includes a reference guide for 130 issues with corresponding skits, music, mimes and movie clips.

STUDYING THE BLUEPRINT

WHAT IS YOUR REACTION?

Distribute writing utensils and copies of the student sheet on page 46 of this book. Give students several minutes to answer the questions. After they have finished, allow a few of them to share their answers. Discuss them, referring to the background material as needed.

Close by saying, **"God did not react to our sin by giving us what we deserved—death. He acted upon his love for us by giving his Son to die on the cross, bearing all our sins on his shoulders."**

Have someone read 1 John 1:9 aloud. Comment, **"When we confess our sins to him, choosing to obey and give our lives to him wholeheartedly, he promises that our lives before him will be 'just as if we never sinned.'"**

Materials needed:
Copies of reproducible student sheet on page 46; Bibles; writing utensils

HARD ACT TO FOLLOW

Before class, cut the reproducible sheet into five strips as indicated. Divide students into five groups and distribute one strip from the student sheet to each of the groups. Have them look up the verses in their Bibles and answer the questions as a group. Discuss the answers, sharing as much background information as time permits.

Conclude by asking the following questions:
- **What do we deserve for our sins?**
- **If we were on trial for our sins and were convicted, what would the punishment be?**

Close with this quote: **"God does not *react* to our sins; he *acted* on them for our behalf."**

Materials needed:
Reproducible student sheet on page 47; Bibles; writing utensils

REMODELING THE INTERIOR

THE BALLOON MAN

Ask the question, **"Is there any sin God will not forgive? No, in 1 John 1:9 God promises to forgive ALL our sins. He is faithful and just and will purify our temples to be used by him when we give him full ownership of our house. We have to hand over the mortgage to him and he pays it in full so we can live eternally with him. It is a promise that is sealed in Christ's blood. How will we react to God's act?"**

Read aloud the following story:

"Everywhere he went, the man carried brightly colored balloons. People at work had grown accustomed to seeing them. Even at night, the balloons would float above the man as he slept. One day, he went to the fair and had a great time. At the fair, he could blend into the atmosphere of the rides, lights and noise. At one of the

Materials needed:
Paper; invisible ink; helium balloons; CD or tape player; the song "Let it Go," by the Newsboys, on their album *Take Me to Your Leader*

booths he filled out an entry form to see if he could win a free ocean cruise. He certainly didn't plan on winning, but it wouldn't hurt to try. Two weeks later a telegram came—he had won! At the dock he was welcomed by the officials who had planned his trip. They even had someone take his suitcases down to his cabin while he stayed on deck and enjoyed the activity. The ship was crowded. Many people were aboard just to say good-bye to friends. Confetti, horns, streamers, and lots of balloons . . . he felt right at home.

Eventually the visitors left and the voyage began. It was great! Someone told the balloon man that the evening meal was in just one hour—a welcome relief because he was hungry! When they rang the bell, he started to walk toward the dining room on the second deck. The aroma of food was so enticing. There was one problem, however. Whoever had designed the ship hadn't left enough room for a man with a handful of balloons to walk down the passageway. You could do it if you released some of the balloons, but the balloon man just couldn't do that. He had seen some crackers and cheese on the upper deck earlier, so he went back and ate that instead. It might not have been as good as the chef's dinner, but it was good enough. Besides, he had his balloons.

That night the sunset was beautiful, but the sea air made him very tired. He asked one of the ship's crew where his room was. The crewman took him down a wide hall and opened the door of his cabin. They had given him one of the classiest rooms on the ship. He could see that the interior decorating was the best. The bed looked inviting. Unfortunately, the door to the cabin wasn't wide enough for him to get all the balloons in without breaking some. He tried, but it just wouldn't work.

Back on deck he found some blankets and a deck chair. He tied the balloons around his wrist and the arm of the chair and tried to sleep. The next morning he was still tired. All that day he ate crackers and cheese. That night he slept on deck again.

The next morning the balloon man received an engraved invitation from the captain of the ship. He had been invited to sit at the captain's table and enjoy the specialty the world-famous chef had prepared especially for the balloon man. All that day the man watched as the crew made preparations for the evening banquet; at 8:00 P.M. the ship's bell rang and the passengers began to go to the dining room. The man watched them go. Soon he could hear the murmur of voices, the sound of silverware and the clink of glasses. The aroma of the food became even more enticing.

He stood at the end of the passageway for some time. Finally he walked to the back of the ship. He could still hear the dinner in progress. He reached in his pocket and felt the engraved invitation. He knew there was a special place reserved for him at the captain's table. Then he looked up at his balloons. It was hard to do, but slowly—very, very slowly (he hadn't unclenched his hand for years)—one at a time he uncurled his fingers. One by one the balloons began to drift away.

As he watched, the wind caught them and blew them out of sight. The man turned and walked down the passageway. That night, as a guest at the captain's table, he enjoyed the finest meal and the best companionship he'd ever known."[1]

After you have read the story, ask:
- **Do you have a handful of balloons that is keeping you from having a relationship with Christ?**
- **What are the names of your balloons? Pride? Sex? Possessions?**

Comment, **"The master wants you to sit at his table. Are you willing to let go?"**

Have the students come up one by one and grab a piece of white paper. Instruct them to write (in invisible ink) a sin they need to let go of so they can have a closer relationship with Christ. Have them tie these to the ends of the balloons. Go outside. Have a prayer. While you play, "Let it Go," by the Newsboys, have them launch their balloons, listening to the song while they watch them float away.

THE ULTIMATE SACRIFICE

Show the portion of the film *Jesus* where Jesus is dying on the cross and the temple curtain is torn. Say, **"When Jesus died on the cross, he became the ultimate sacrifice for our sins. He took all of our sins to the cross with him. Maybe you've cheated on your test—it is there. Maybe you've gone too far on a date—it is there. He carried them *all* to the cross, causing God, who could not be in the presence of sin, to turn his back on his Son because of your sin. That is why Jesus cried out, 'My God, my God, why have you forsaken me?' How do we react to that act of love? We clean house. We ask the bearer of our sin to forgive us of our sins. There is no other way to have a temple ready to be occupied by God."**

Have a candle lit on a stool or a table close by you. Pick up a piece of flash paper. Have someone read Hebrews 10:17, 18. Then say, **"Jesus became the ultimate sacrifice so our sins could be remembered no more."** Light the flash paper and throw it up in the air. Comment, **"There is no trace of the flash paper. It was completely consumed. In the same way, God forgives our sin. We ask for forgiveness, he forgives it and it is gone, no longer to be remembered. The test you cheated on . . .** (light a flash paper). **He remembers it no more. The time in the back seat . . .** (light a flash paper). **He remembers it no more."**

Distribute a piece of flash paper to each student. Have them write on the paper a sin that they want God to remember no more. Instruct them to come up one at a time and light the flash paper and throw it up into the air. As they do, play the song, "Make It a Promise," by Clay Crosse. It is recorded on the album, *Utmost for His Highest II*. Stress that this is a commitment to God by saying, **"God has fulfilled his part of the promise by sending his Son to die. What are we going to do to fulfill our part of that promise? How will we react to his act?"**

Distribute copies of **The Midweek Clean** to your students.

Materials needed:
TV; VCR; the movie *Jesus*, by Jesus Films Productions; flash paper; writing utensils; candle; matches; CD or tape player; the song "Make It a Promise," by Clay Crosse

Check This . . .
This could be a very important time for those that have not received Christ as their Savior. Invite anyone who has not made that decision to talk with you after class.

WHAT IS YOUR REACTION?

Have you ever been thrown an object as someone yelled, "Think fast!"? How quickly did you react? Describe the reaction in the following situations:

How would your parents react if . . .
• You got an "F" on a report card?

• You were found alone in a dark room with a member of the opposite sex?

How would your best friend react if . . .
• He/she shared something personal with you and you told someone else?

• You stole their boyfriend or girlfriend?

How would you react if . . .
• Someone close to you made a promise to do something with you or for you and then forgot to do it?

• What if he or she *chose* not to do it?

Read Ezra 9:1-6. How did Ezra react to the sins of Israel? What was their sin?

We can learn from Israel's example of how they reacted to their sin to help us restore our relationship with God. Read the following verses from Ezra 10 and fill in the blanks.

v. 2 The Israelites *recognized* their sin as being _____.

vv. 2, 3 They *realized* their sin was _____

vv. 1, 11 They *reacted* to their sin by _____.

v. 17 They *rid* themselves of what was hindering their relationship with God by _____
_____.

Read Zechariah 9:9. They *replaced* it with a promise of _____ coming.

Read Romans 6:23. God should *react* to our sin by punishing us with _____ but
he gives us _____ instead.

HARD ACT TO FOLLOW

Read Ezra 6:3-11. How does God react when his temple is not taken care of and used properly?

GROUP ONE

Read Ezra 6:13-22. How did the Israelites react when the temple was completed?

GROUP TWO

Read Ezra 7:8-28. How did Ezra know how to react to God
when called by him to lead the third group back to Israel?

GROUP THREE

How did the king of Persia react when Ezra asked to go? Why did he react that way? (v. 27)

Read Ezra 9:1-13; 10:1-17. How did Ezra react when he discovered Israel's sin?

GROUP FOUR

How did the people respond to Ezra's reaction?

Read Ezra 8:22. How does God react to Israel's sin and ours?

GROUP FIVE

Read Romans 6:23. What punishment do we deserve for our sins?

The Midweek Clean
A Guide for Remodeling the Interior

Something to Read

Take a few moments to reread Ezra 9. Then read Hebrews 10:19-39.

Something to Think About

- Compare Ezra 9 to Hebrews 10:26-32. Why do you think the Israelites continued to sin even after everything they went through in captivity and in building the temple?

- What one word in Hebrews 10:32 will help us stand our ground? (It is an eight-letter word that begins with "r".) What is it that we are suppose to "r . . . . . ."?

- In Hebrews 10:25, 37, 38, it tells about the day of Christ's return. According to verses 19-39, what are some things we can do to keep us going (persevere) until he returns?

- How important are other Christians in this?

- If I continue sinning, how will this affect my ability to stay strong to the end?

- Where do we get the confidence to continue living the Christian life?

- What is our reward? What did Christ promise?

Something to Do

Ask someone trustworthy to be your accountability partner, someone who knows your struggles and can keep up on how you are doing. Choose someone who is nonjudgmental, who will encourage you and pray for you. Decide a time daily in which you can have a one-minute prayer with someone at a locker. Encourage someone else by sending a Scripture note to them once a week.

"'Here we are before you in our guilt, though because of it not one of us can stand in your presence.'" Ezra 9:15

HIGH MAINTENANCE BUT WELL WORTH THE COST

LAYING THE FOUNDATION

EZRA 9:1, 2; 10

Ezra was pretty shocked when he showed up in Israel to find the temple built but the inner temple still in need of repair. The same old sin, the one that put them into captivity, made its way around again. The Israelite men married wives from the surrounding countries, which means they also married their idols. Ezra cried out to God, throwing himself down before the temple. The people saw this and they also began to cry. Realizing their unfaithfulness, the leaders decided to make a covenant to send away all the wives and their children who were not worshiping the one and only God. They also put Ezra in charge of the investigation to determine who fit into that category.

A huge assembly was called, mandating all the exiles to attend or they would lose their possessions and rights to the temple. The exiles stood outside in the pouring rain to hear Ezra tell them that they had messed up again, "'Fess up and separate." They responded, "You are right!" Not all the people agreed to send their wives away (10:15). But when it comes to obeying God, it is not necessary to agree with him. Our job is to just do it! "So the exiles did as was proposed" (10:16). It seemed pretty harsh to send away women and children, but God knew what had to be done to purify Israel. If this action was not enforced, the nation would eventually fade away, disturbing the lineage of Christ.

This chapter reminds us that we are all susceptible to mess-ups; they are a part of life. For some reason, God does not give up on us. He keeps promising, but we keep compromising. We need to learn to maintain our relationship with Christ by separating ourselves from the things that hurt our walk with him.

EZRA 8:28

As Christians, we are consecrated to God. According to *The Random House Dictionary*, the word consecrated means "something that is declared sacred or dedicated to God for a particular purpose." We are precious to God. He declares us sacred! We need to guard our temples carefully, dedicating them to God with our every word and action.

LESSON TEXT
Ezra 8:28; 9:1, 2; 10

LESSON FOCUS
"You as well as these articles are consecrated to the LORD. . . . Guard them carefully . . ." Ezra 8:28, 29

LESSON GOALS
As a result of participating in this lesson, students will:
- Realize that the Israelites continued to struggle with keeping their commitment to God.
- Believe that after they accept God's forgiveness, they must also separate themselves from the habits and people that are leading them to sin.
- Discover the spiritual furnishings that God fills his "temple" with so it can be maintained until Christ comes.
- Be encouraged with the news that we will be in the full presence of God in Heaven.

2 CORINTHIANS 6:14-18; 7:1

These verses explain that we should not be yoked with unbelievers (yoked means "to be joined to"). This does not mean that we should deny friendships with non-Christians. If that was the case, then how could we ever share our faith in Jesus? This teaching from the apostle Paul means not to be joined with them by following their example, participating in their actions or compromising our beliefs to follow their "gods."

The second greatest commandment is to love others. Yet we are to love others without contaminating ourselves and diluting our beliefs. Contamination occurs when something pure comes in contact with or is mixed with something impure. The key word is "mixed." As Christians, we become contaminated when we no longer stand on God's truth, compromising our beliefs to act and think contrary to his Word. When we experience life in the purest form by having a relationship with the one and living God, what reason could there be to give it up? God asks for all or nothing.

SKETCHING THE DESIGN

1 SQUEAKY CLEAN! NOW WHAT?

Begin this activity by saying, **"I have two glasses with me today. They are very clean. I washed them in hot, soapy water. I rinsed them in bleach water to sterilize them, and then I blow-dried the inside so I would not contaminate them. They are ready to be used. What if I decided not to use them? I could just set them on this table and leave them empty. What would eventually happen? Would they get dirty just from the air around them? Would they serve the purpose they were created for? No. I didn't go to all that work to just let them sit. So what will I fill them with?"**

Grab Jug #1 and pour the contents into a glass. Ask, **"What happened to my nice sterile glass? In order for me to use this sterilized glass and keep it sterilized, I would have to pour clean water into it."** Pour the water from Jug #2 into the other glass. **"From which glass would you drink?"**

Continue by saying, **"In our Christian lives, we often do this. Christ purifies us from sin. Then we fill our temple right back up with bad habits that eventually lead to sin. When we sin, we must go through an emptying process. First we separate ourselves from that sin** (empty the dirty glass), **confess it to God** (wash and dry the glass) **and then fill our lives with Christlike contents that only God provides** (fill the glass with the sterile water). **The last chapter of Ezra explains how the Israelites' constant struggle with the same sin taught them a valuable lesson on what was necessary to keep their inside temple unpolluted."**

Materials needed:
Two clean, clear drinking glasses; a jug of dirty water (as gross as possible) marked "Jug #1"; a jug of clean, sterilized water (bottled water for babies) marked "Jug #2"; an empty bowl; a bowl with hot, soapy water; a clean washcloth; towel

Check This . . .
Another option you might consider is to draw a large heart on a poster board. Write this statement in the middle of the heart: "Love God with all of your heart, then . . ." As your students enter, have them write an ending to the sentence around the heart. When everyone has had the opportunity to write, finish the sentence by writing inside the heart, "Love God with all of your heart, then . . . do whatever you want." Ask for comments on why or why not this is true. Then ask, **"As Christians, why can't we live like we want and just ask forgiveness later?"**

JULIA CHILD'S EGGZASPERATION

Ask for a volunteer who would be willing to separate an egg into two bowls. Instruct the volunteer to separate one of the eggs, putting the white of the egg in one bowl and the yolk in the other. That person is to give step-by-step directions as if she were Julia Child teaching a class. She can even talk like her if she desires.

When the volunteer is finished, ask students, **"What had to take place to make this egg separated?"** Ask the volunteer to take the separated egg and put the two parts together in the same bowl. Now ask, **"Is it still separated? Is it in the same form as before?"** Request that the volunteer pour the egg back into the shell, using transparency tape to put it back together and make it whole again.

Ask, **"Is it possible to put the egg in the same form as before? Why not? Why would we want to? As silly as this seems, many Christians try to do the same thing. They ask God to forgive them, but then they try to fit their style of living in the same mold as before. Today we are going to learn the same lesson the Israelites learned back in Ezra's day—how to separate from the world and how to maintain a Christian temple."**

Studying the Blueprint

IT'S MOVING DAY!

Distribute writing utensils and copies of the student sheet on page 54 of this book to your students. Divide them into two groups. Ask one group to complete the "Empty House" side and the other the "Full House" side. When they have finished, discuss the background of the material, referring to the commentary.

Conclude this activity by saying, **"God's power is like the electricity in our homes. It flows constantly. He has furnished us with spiritual appliances. To make those appliances work, we must plug into the power. Ephesians 1:19, 20 states that the same power that raised Jesus from the dead is available to us today to maintain our temple. It is not by our efforts that we are able to live the Christian life but by God's power that flows through us."**

TOOL TIME!

Begin by saying, **"The routine spiritual maintenance of our temple is not an easy task. If we are slack in the daily, nonstop upkeep, even just a little, the end result could be a real mess. Let's look at the Israelites and the lesson they learned in 'Maintenance 101.'"** Read Ezra 10:1-17 aloud as a group. Discuss the text by referring to the commentary. Then ask:

- **With what sin were the Israelites struggling? Did they ever struggle with this sin before?** (Refer to 2 Chronicles 36:14, 20 if necessary)

Materials needed:
Two or three eggs; two small bowls; roll of transparency tape; a damp towel

Check This . . .
Egg Toss!
For something different, try an old-fashioned egg toss. Provide each student with a large trash bag with a slit cut in the bottom, large enough to fit a head through. Divide into pairs with each team facing each other. Have one person stay in one place and the other move a step backwards after each toss of the egg. When everyone is a mess, ask: **"What kept the egg from breaking? Why was it harder to catch the egg the farther you got away from your partner? Why is it harder to follow God the farther we get away from his Word? Failing to follow God closely can also lead to a messy life."**

Materials needed:
Copies of the reproducible student sheet on page 54; writing utensils

Check This . . .
An excellent song that brings out the focus of this lesson is "Takes a Little Time," by Amy Grant. It is recorded on her album *Behind the Eyes*.

Materials needed:
Copies of the reproducible student sheet on page 55; writing utensils

Check This . . .
This would be another good spot to show a brief clip of the sitcom *Home Improvement*. Begin at a spot where Tim and Al are presenting their TV show *Tool Time*. Tim seems to always desire to hurry the building process by tampering with the tools to make them more powerful, usually resulting in a mess. God provides the right tools, at the right time, with the right amount of power. We just need to trust him and his power.

Materials needed:
Reproducible student sheet on page 56; writing utensils

Check This . . .
"What Do I Do the Next Time I Sin?"
1. *Evaluate*: Why was it wrong? Why did you do it? What action, thought or person contributed to that sin?
2. *Ask* for forgiveness. Then accept it.
3. *Plug* into the power of the Holy Spirit and God's Word.
4. *Flee* from tempting circumstances.
5. *Seek* help from other Christians to hold you accountable and pray for you.
6. *Remember* sin is only temporary, but God is eternal.

Materials needed:
Reproducible student sheet on page 56; writing utensils

- **What did Ezra and the leaders command the people to do to finally get rid of this problem? Did the people do it?**
- **Is God surprised when we mess up?** *(No, because we are only human. We cannot maintain our own building. It is impossible. Because of that, God provides tools for us to maintain our house until the day we are with him in Heaven.)*

Comment, **"Let's take a moment to look at these tools and how to use them."**

Divide your students into four groups and assign each group a different tool to research in the Bible. Pass out writing utensils and copies of the reproducible student sheet on page 55 of this book. After they have had enough time to complete their study, allow a spokesperson from each group to report back to everyone. Discuss the different tools that God has given us to maintain our temple.

REMODELING THE INTERIOR

HEAVENLY FEELING!

Begin by saying, **"Another important piece of furniture to fill our house with is God's promise of eternal life in Heaven."** Have someone read Revelation 21:22-27; 22:3, 4. Ask, **"Why will there not be a temple in Heaven? We will not only be in the presence of God, but we will see him face to face. That alone is reason enough to maintain our temple for him."**

Pass out copies of the reproducible student sheet entitled, "The Contract." Say, **"Whether you are going to buy, remodel or rent a home, you are required to sign a contract with someone to seal an agreement. Throughout these lessons you have learned what it means to be a cleansed temple of God and what is needed to maintain it until Christ returns. Read over 'The Contract.' If you agree to its terms, sign your name at the bottom. Then take it home and post it somewhere to constantly remind yourself of your agreement with God."**

Have a prayer circle thanking God for providing us with the power and equipment to maintain our lives for him.

THE MASTER PAINTER

Comment, **"It is not the mess-ups in our life that God is concerned about. He is more concerned when we do not trust him to use those mistakes as tools for his trade. God *can* and *will* work around and through our humanness. Our sin is like a painter who goes to paint a wall. He paints the entire wall until he comes to a box against the wall. He is in a hurry to finish, so, instead of moving the box he paints around it. It looks pretty good if you don't move the box. The master builder sees the error and shows the painter. Yes, the painter messed up but, realizing his error, he confesses it to the master builder and asks for help.**

Does the master builder fire the man? No, the master builder helps him.

First they move the box together. Then, using his expert knowledge, the master builder paints the bare spot on the wall, smoothing it perfectly to blend in with the other paint. The master builder does not stop there; he proceeds to paint the box too and then he pays the painter for a job well done. God, our Master Builder, does incredibly more in our life than we could ever imagine.

Our life and our temple have nothing to do with us, our abilities or our lack of them. It has everything to do with God's power and his ability to maintain our lives. It is not what we can do for God, but rather what he can do through our human temples. When we allow God to accomplish this through us, he gets the glory and we get the blessing. Pretty incredible, huh?"

Distribute writing utensils and copies of the "The Contract." Repeat the same instructions that are listed in the previous activity. Distribute copies of **The Midweek Clean** to your students.

Check This . . .
Instead of having the students take their contract home, mail it to them later. Pass out an envelope to each student. Ask them to sign the contract, then seal it in the envelope. Tell them to write their name and address on the outside. Be sure to mail it to them in a couple of months.

IT'S MOVING DAY!

After centuries of planning, sparing no cost for remodeling and cleaning, it is time for the owner to move in. God, desiring to settle in and really enjoy his house, has hired an interior decorator, the Holy Spirit, to furnish his house.

The Israelites had to empty their spiritual temple of old furniture that had been collecting dust for years. Read these verses and write down what they had to move out, so God could move in.

• What sin were the Israelites struggling with and why was it wrong? (Ezra 9:1, 2)

• Did the Israelites ever struggle with this sin before? When? What happened the last time they had this problem? (2 Chronicles 36:14, 20)

• Who brought this problem to their attention and what did he suggest they do about it? (Ezra 10:3, 4, 10-14, 16)

• What did the people do about it? (Ezra 10:10-14, 16)

• Did all the people agree? (Ezra 10:15)

• Did the Israelites take care of the problem anyway? (Ezra 10:16, 17)

Below is the Holy Spirit's checklist of what we need to fill our temple with to make us a worthy place to house the living God. Read these verses and answer the questions below.

☐ Galatians 5:22-25

☐ 1 Thessalonians 2:13

☐ 2 Peter 1:3-11

☐ Ephesians 3:14-21

What is your greatest motivation to live a clean and holy life?

a) my love for God, to please him

b) God's love for me, even though I don't deserve it

c) my fear of God, not to be punished

d) my own self-respect, to be true to myself

e) my parents, not to disappoint them

f) my friends, not to let them down

Which one of these motivations will actually empower you to maintain your temple?

TOOL TIME!

Featuring the Holy Spirit and His Power Tools

Read the verses below and determine what each of these power tools do.

Drill

1 Thessalonians 2:13

1 Corinthians 2:10-16

Screwdriver

James 5:16

Romans 8:26, 27

Sander

Romans 8:28

Philippians 2:13

Power Saw

Ephesians 1:19-21

Ephesians 3:14-21

"Greater is He that is in me, than he that is in the world." 1 John 4:4 (*KJV*)

THE CONTRACT

This is an agreement, sealed with the blood of Christ, between God the Creator, and _____, a temple.

I realize that I am a temple of God built by his design to glorify him with my life, actions and words.

I realize that God provides me with the power and tools, such as the Holy Spirit, the Word of God, prayer and people to help me maintain my temple.

I promise to rely on those tools to separate myself from the thoughts, actions and people that are leading me to sin.

I understand that as a human structure, I will continue to struggle but I will constantly remember who owns me, realizing that God's presence lives inside me.

I will remember that God can use anything that happens in my life, even my mess-ups, and make good come from it.

My desire is to stand on a solid foundation until the day I will stand in the full presence of God.

Signed,

_____

A Holy Dwelling of God

The Midweek Clean
A Guide for Remodeling the Interior

Something to Read

Take a few moments to read 2 Peter 1:3-11.

Something to Think About

What has God's power equipped us with? (v. 3)

What happens if we do not possess these qualities? (v. 8)

If we do not have them, what have we forgotten? (v. 9)

If we do these things, what will not happen? (v. 10)

What kind of welcome will we receive in God's house someday? (v. 11)

Something to Do

Read verses five through seven again. Using one color, circle the qualities that you feel God has increased in your life. With another color, circle the qualities that you need God to help with. If your Bible has a reference section in the back, turn to it now and look up those qualities that require more help. Write down the verses that are listed next to those qualities. Keep these on a 3" x 5" card to remind you daily of God's construction in your life.

"To this end I labor, struggling with all his energy, which so powerfully works in me." Colossians 1:29

BONUS SESSION

ROCK THE HOUSE WORSHIP

TEXT
Ephesians 2:19-22; 1 Peter 2:4-10

FOCUS
To provide an opportunity for teenagers to join together as one dwelling to worship God creatively.

Before Christ came to earth, people would enter a structure to be near the presence of God and worship him. Today, it is reversed. The presence of God, living in his redeemed people, enters the structure to be worshiped.

From a glance, being a temple seems fairly individualized. We realize we need to be cleansed of our sin, we ask God to cleanse us, he does so and we maintain our temple by filling it with godliness through the power of the Holy Spirit. With so much happening on the inside, it is easy to forget our mutual reliance on other Christians. Seeing it from God's point of view, each individual temple is only one stone in a larger dwelling called his kingdom, the church. One stone is useless without the other. In allowing Christ to "clean house" of sins individually, Christians become etched in intricate detail to custom-fit the other stones to create the church. The Bible says when two or more are gathered, he is also there (Matthew 18:20). He is there because his redeemed people are there. And when they are joined together with their focus completely on him, there is an outpouring of his blessings.

In Ezra 6:19-22 the Israelites had a worship service. First, they purified themselves according to God's law. They became ceremonially clean, joining "together with all who had separated themselves" in order to seek out the Lord. Then they celebrated what God had accomplished in their lives because he had filled them with joy. When we become Christians, we become ceremonially clean according to God's Word and his plan carried out through Jesus Christ. Our response to what God has accomplished in our lives should be pure worship.

THE DESIGN OF THE WORSHIP SERVICE

The worship service suggested here is designed to provide your students with different aspects of worship, allowing them to choose the style of how those aspects will be carried out. Two different worship service options are presented for your consideration. Each one contains instructions and a time frame to complete it. Use this time with your students not to just bring closure to the *Rock the House* study but to worship the great God of the Bible, thanking him for the many results he has accomplished through it. When God cleans house of sin and his Word is let loose in lives, change always occurs.

SPONTANEOUS WORSHIP

A. BEFORE YOU BEGIN

- Arrange to have the worship service in a large outdoor place such as a church camp or a state park. Try to provide transportation to this spot. If a large area is not possible, choose a time when the entire church facilities are available.
- Instruct the students beforehand either by announcement or via postcard that their Bibles are required for this event.
- Read over the Scriptures on the student sheet so that you can answer any questions that might arise.
- Cut the student sheet into strips.
- Provide communion cups, juice and bread if the students choose to do communion the traditional way.
- Pray for guidance.

Materials needed:
One copy of the reproducible student sheet on page 62, cut into strips

B. TIME FRAME

The time required for this bonus session is at least two hours for the actual lesson, worship preparation time and worship.

C. TEACHING

Gather the students together in a small area. Ask them, **"Why do we give gifts? If you could give God any gift, what would that gift be?"** After they have responded, ask, **"What have you learned about yourself and your relationship with Christ during this study of Ezra? What gift has God given you? Today we are going to give God a gift by worshiping him. Worship is our response to who God is and what he has accomplished in our lives."**

Have someone read Ephesians 2:19-22. Discuss how we are individual dwellings of God but he builds us together to be one holy temple, the church. Then have someone read 1 Peter 2:4-10, and discuss how we are like "living stones" built together into a spiritual house. The result is that we may declare the praises of him who has called us out of darkness into his wonderful light—in other words, worship!

D. WORSHIP PREPARATIONS

Instruct your students that the worship service that will take place is spontaneous and requires spiritual creativity on their part. The service is broken down into six parts. Students will be divided into six groups. Each group will be responsible for one part of the worship service.

Inform students that they are not required to do their part in the traditional way but can if they choose to do so. For example, communion is traditionally observed by a sharing of a devotion, followed by the partaking of juice and a cracker. But the word "communion" actually means "a sharing, as of thoughts and emotions." Therefore, the group that is responsible for communion may want to omit the traditional way and instruct the rest of the group "to share with Christ" in another creative way. One possibility might be for them to go off alone for one-on-one time with Christ to reflect on what he did for them on the cross. Or this could be done in addition to the traditional way.

Divide the students into their groups. Give each group a slip of paper from the student sheet that describes its particular area of responsibility. They are to read the instructions and follow the guidelines found there. Inform them of the actual time the worship service will begin. Each group is to check in with you before the service begins so its plans are approved by you. Be flexible. Allow the teens to express to God what is on the inside of their temples. But do not allow the groups to be so flexible that the meaning of worship is taken too lightly. When this worship service is pulled off in the right context, the results can be pretty amazing.

 # PLANNED WORSHIP

A. BEFORE YOU BEGIN

Materials needed:
One copy of the reproducible student sheet on page 62, cut into strips

- Read over the Scriptures on the student sheet so that you can answer any questions that might arise.
- Cut the student sheet into strips.
- Make a list of the students in attendance, their phone numbers and their areas of responsibility.
- Keep a record of what has already been accomplished, supplies needed and what still needs to be done.
- Provide transportation on the day of the worship service, if needed.
- Pray for guidance.

B. TIME FRAME

Two separate times will be needed for this worship experience; one time to meet and plan the worship service with your teens and another for the actual service to take place. Allow at least one hour for each meeting.

C. FIRST MEETING

Materials needed:
Student sheet cut into strips; paper; writing utensils; calendar

Set up a time to meet with your students. Inform them that they will need their Bibles for the meeting.

- **TEACHING**

When your students gather for this meeting, take at least 15 minutes to share with them about worship. To get them thinking, ask,

"**What does the word 'worship' mean to you? What things do we worship other than God? The common Greek word for worship in the New Testament is** *proskuneo,* **which means 'to kiss toward, to kiss the hand, to bow down.' How can we show these actions to God?**" Read Ephesians 2:9-12 and 1 Peter 2:4-10, discussing how we are temples that are joined together as one holy dwelling—the church.

- **WORSHIP PREPARATIONS**

Instruct your students that they are to plan a worship experience that will take place at a later time. It will require spiritual creativity on their part. The worship service is broken down into five parts. They will be divided into five groups, each group being responsible for one part of the worship service. Tell them that they are not required to do their part in the traditional way but can if they choose to do so. For example, communion is traditionally observed by a sharing of a devotion, followed by the partaking of juice and crackers. The word "communion" actually means "a sharing, as of thoughts and emotions." That sharing is with Christ. Therefore, the group that is responsible for this may want to omit the traditional way and instruct the rest of the group in a different way to share with Christ. This could be by going off alone for one-on-one time with Christ to reflect on what he did for them on the cross. Or, this could be done in addition to the traditional way.

Before you divide them into their groups, discuss the date that this worship service will take place. You can set up this date yourself or have them plan that as well. Divide them into groups, giving each group the slip of paper that describes its particular area of responsibility. Give them as much time as needed to discuss and to plan. Check in with each group periodically to guide them in their plans. When they are finished, bring them together and discuss the plans as an entire group, making a list of what needs to be done in order to get ready. Take the time for the students to carry out as much of the plans as possible, making necessary calls and gathering supplies. If there are additional items on their list that cannot be taken care of at the time, reminder calls, by you, might be necessary throughout the week to ensure that commitments are taken care of. Set up a time to meet early just before the service to make final preparations.

All plans should be approved by you to ensure this worship service will be as meaningful as possible. Be flexible. Allow the teens to be able to use this worship service to express to God what is on the inside of their temples. But do not allow the groups to be so flexible that the meaning of worship is taken too lightly. Then, sit back, or stand up—and watch what God can do through your teens!

D. SECOND MEETING— THE WORSHIP EXPERIENCE

Meet early enough to go over any last-minute preparations. Greet those whom you have invited to your service as they enter your place of meeting. Then . . . *Rock the House* in worship!

Check This . . .
You may want to make this worship service available to the adults or use it as a guide for a Youth Sunday. Have the students announce the time and place or pass out flyers. Use it as an evangelistic tool by inviting other teens.

PURE WORSHIP

Group #1—Place of Worship/Order of Events
First read John 4:21-24.

Your responsibility is to choose a place for the worship experience that will ensure "true worshipers will worship the Father in spirit and truth." Prepare the place as desired with logs or chairs. Your other responsibility is to check with each of the other groups to plan the order of worship. Inform the other groups of the schedule and when the worship service begins, you will help facilitate the flow.

Group #2—Music and Praise
First read Psalm 150:3-6; Nehemiah 12:27-31, 40.

Your responsibility is to provide music and praise for the worship service. This can be accomplished through songs, instruments, a worship band, taped music, solos, a choir, poetry or drama. Ask God to give you creativity. This plays an extremely important part in honoring God in our worship. So, consider prayerfully your choices.

Group #3—Scripture Reading and teaching
First read 1 Timothy 4:9-13.

Your responsibility is to provide a biblical truth in the worship service. This can be accomplished in the form of teaching, preaching, devotion, reading a Scripture, a sharing time, etc. Be creative but do not take this lightly, for God might have a message for the rest of the group that he wants to be said through you.

Group #4—Prayer
First read James 5:13-16.

Your responsibility for the worship service is more than just praying at the beginning and at the end of the service. You may want to provide a five-minute personal prayer time in the middle of the service or have a prayer circle at the end where everyone in the entire group says a one-word prayer. Be creative and make it as meaningful as possible; remember who you are going to be talking to—the Creator of the universe.

Group #5—Giving
First read Psalm 51:15-17; Romans 12:1.

Your responsibility for the worship service is to provide an opportunity to the rest of the group to provide an offering. Offering does not necessarily have to be monetary. Offering is a way of offering back a portion of what God has given to us. Think of what God has given to this group lately that a portion of it could be given back. In what form could it be given back? Be creative.

Group #6—Communion
First read 1 Corinthians 11:23-28; Hebrews 9:11-14, 22.

Your responsibility is to provide a time of communion for the rest of the group. The word "communion" actually means "a sharing, as of thoughts and emotions." For a Christian, that sharing is with Christ, remembering what he did on the cross for us. Make this a very special time.

NOTES

LESSON 2

[1]*Life Application® Bible,* ©1988, 1989, 1990, 1991, by Tyndale House Publishers, Inc. Wheaton, Il 60189. All rights reserved.

LESSON 4

[1]*Life Application® Bible,* ©1988, 1989, 1990, 1991, by Tyndale House Publishers, Inc. Wheaton, Il 60189. All rights reserved.

LESSON 5

[1]Reprinted from *More Hot Illustrations for Youth Talks,* copyright 1996 by Youth Specialties, Inc. 1224 Greenfield Dr., El Cajon, CA 92021. Used by permission.

OTHER EMPOWERED YOUTH PRODUCTS FROM STANDARD PUBLISHING

SOME KIND OF JOURNEY
On the Road With Audio Adrenaline

By Jim Burgen, Ginny McCabe, and Dale Reeves

Seven strangers from across the country teamed up to spend a week on the road with one of today's hottest Christian bands, Audio Adrenaline. Why? To talk about seven relevant issues that concern today's youth—such as depression, sex, prejudice and divorce. Includes an AudioVision CD that features interactive discussions, songs, videos and more! You'll also get behind-the-scenes tour photos of the band and the seven people who journeyed with them.
Order number 26-03304 (ISBN 0-7847-0744-8)

NO ACCIDENT . . . NO APOLOGIES
Helping Teens Understand the Creation/Evolution Debate

By Geoff Moore and Jim Eichenberger

This six-session video curriculum features a 40-minute video hosted by contemporary Christian artist Geoff Moore. Guide your teens in exploring what the Bible says about the creation account and the importance of standing boldly for God in their schools. In addition to a leader's guide, reproducible student sheets and a bonus music video are also included.
Order number 26-03308 (ISBN 0-7847-0788-X)

WHY BE NORMAL?
A Creative Study of the Sermon on the Mount

By Michael Warden

This six-session elective for junior-high and senior-high teens will help them ignite their world by living out Christ's challenge in Matthew 5-7. Each session features reproducible student sheets, contemporary Christian music suggestions, numerous options and a midweek challenge. A bonus event gives youth the opportunity to "take the dare" and share Christ publicly.
Order number 26-23309 (ISBN 0-7847-0769-3)

40 DAYS WITH GOD
A Devotional Journey
With Rebecca St. James

Australian-born Rebecca St. James shares her personal walk with God in this inspiring devotional. Includes 40 devotions in a spiral-bound journal and features scrapbook photos of this Grammy- and Dove-nominated Christian singer. Comes with a bonus AudioVision CD with interviews, three videos and five songs.
Order number 26-23303 (ISBN 0-7847-0569-0)

TO ORDER, CONTACT YOUR LOCAL CHRISTIAN BOOKSTORE.
(IF THE BOOK IS OUT OF STOCK, YOU CAN ORDER BY CALLING 1-800-543-1353.)